The Flower of Battle
MS Ludwig XV 13

The Flower of Battle
MS Ludwig XV 13

TRANSLATED BY – COLIN HATCHER
FORMATTING – TRACY MELLOW
Copyright 2017, All Rights Reserved

ISBN 13 978-0-9847716-8-4
ISBN 10 0-9847716-8-9

Special thanks to the Getty Museum which has made their art available though the Getty Open Content program.

History Commentary
Richard Marsden

In the 13th to the 15th century Italy as we know it today did not exist. The peninsula was divided into city-states, petty kingdoms and riddled with factions. The nobles were set against the wealthy guildsmen, the pro-Papal Guelphs and the pro-Imperial Ghibellinies were at one another's throats and family vendettas would be the stuff of Shakespeare. The streets of the city were not safe, with Florence boasting a murder-rate twice that of America's most dangerous cities today, and the roads were the domain of bandits and robber-barons. War was ever-present, both within Italy's borders and outside it where the Hundred Years War between England and France ebbed and flowed.

This was the world of Fiore dei Liberi, the son of an Imperial knight, who was born around 1340 and likely died within the first two decades of the 15th century. Fiore was a weapons-master who, for the sake of posterity, set his martial art down in a manuscript entitled, Fior di Battaglia, the Flower of Battle. Much of what we know about Fiore comes from the man himself and his fifty years of experience in teaching, fighting, and dueling.

Of himself, he says he was the son of Free Knight, meaning an Imperial knight who owed his allegiance directly to the Emperor rather than some local lord. He says he wanted to learn everything one could about combat, both in and out of armor, on foot and mounted, with weapons and unarmed.

To learn these arts Fiore traveled extensively to various provinces and cities, learning from Italian and German masters as well as their students. In particular he notes Johane, called Suveno, who was a student of Nicholai of Tolbem. Additionally, Fiore says he was taught by princes, dukes, marquis, and counts, and spent a great deal of time and money learning his art.

Fiore also makes mention that he learned from his own students, who were not novices. These students were trained for mortal combat, but also for a less risky form of combat called fighting at the barrier. Of Fiore's students who dueled at the barrier, he claims none ever lost.

When a pair of knights quarreled, they could ask to fight a public duel which was known as fighting in the barriers- named for the wooden fence that kept the fighters contained in an area. These were expensive, well-publicized affairs. One of Fiore's students, Galeazzo, fought a French knight by the name of Boucicaut in front of an audience of 12,000 people. They met twice, with the first duel in 1395 being called off after Galeazzo scored a hit and Boucicaut sought an axe, and the second time in 1406 where Galeazzo was victorious. Both were celebrated military men in their day. Boucicaut was renowned for his physical prowess and hot-headed nature. He was captured at the battle of Agincourt in 1415 fighting against the English and died in England awaiting ransom at the age of fifty-five.

Galeazzo was typical of Fiore's students. A man who considered himself noble and made his living as a professional soldier, or mercenary, called a condottiere. Fiore was no stranger to mercenaries. The Hundred Years War provided legions of them, both French, English, as well as German to be traded about between Italy's many principalities and cities. Italians produced their own mercenaries, some of which were students of Fiore.

Fiore himself was a mercenary, having raised troops for the nobles of Udine to resist a newly appointed Bishop-Prince of Aquila. The city leaders of Udine also gave him other tasks including inspecting the city's defenses and acting as a magistrate and keeper of the peace.

His ability to teach and his military experience won him patrons and Fiore was known as a perfect master, which brought him into contact with jealous rivals. Fiore says he had to fight jealous masters in five separate duels. These duels were conducted with no armor other than a padded jacket and gloves, and with sharp and pointed swords. Fiore does not say if he killed his opponents, only that he came away with his honor intact and entirely unscathed.

Fiore tells us that one of his own students, Galeazzo da Montova, noted that without books the art could not be known. Fiore took the advice to heart. After fifty years of learning the art of combat, sometime around 1409, Fiore decided to write down and illustrate what he knew. Ever secretive, he does caution his readers not to teach his art to the peasants!

The original Flower of Battle by Fiore dei Liberi is likely lost, but four copies remain. They were created, at great expense, in the early 1400s and were dedicated to Niccolò III d'Este, Marquis of Ferrara, Modena, and Parma- one of the petty kingdoms in Northern Italy.

It is unclear if Fiore was in the court of the d'Este and that the prince wanted the manuscripts made, or if Fiore was in the employ of some other court and they were gifts. It is even unclear if Fiore was involved directly in any of the surviving copies' creation, though judging by the variations of their introductions and what collector and researcher Brian Stokes says are corrections of the artwork, the answer is probably yes.

Of the four surviving copies, Jay Leccese, an art historian, studied them and noted artistic choices that could be seen that suggest an order of their creation.

The likely first manuscript is Ludwig XV 13 known as the Getty (for the museum that holds it) and what this book will replicate. The Getty has detailed illustrations and actual gold worked into the pages, giving a sense of its worth. One does not draw with gold lightly!

The other manuscripts are the Morgan, the Pisani Dossi and the Paris. These were likely made afterwards and influenced by the Getty.

The Getty is the most complete version of the Flower of Battle with the most illustrations as well as the most text. It provides a solid view of Fiore dei Liberi's art and is a cornerstone in today's Historical European Martial Arts.

The area circled in red is where Fiore dei Liberi was most active and likely learned his art. France, with its Hundred Years War to the west and the Holy Roman Empire to the north provided Italy with mercenaries, while endless squabbles on the peninsula spawned local condottieri and plenty of work. Image courtesy Wikicommons, Gabagool.

Statue of the condottieri Bartolomeo Colleoni who was active in the years after Fiore's death. Mercenaries were a staple of Italian politics long past Fiore's lifetime. They could blur the lines between captain-for-hire, bandit, and prince. Image courtesy Wikicommons, Novellón.

Richard Marsden is the author of Polish Saber, Historical European Martial Arts in its Context, and other assorted works, is co-founder of the Phoenix Society of Historical Swordsmanship, was President of the HEMA Alliance and holds a Masters Degree in Land Warfare courtesy AMU. He is very grateful for all the work Colin Hatcher did in translating this work, Tracy Mellow did to format it, and Henry Snider who lovingly makes sure it can go to print with a nice cover!

TYRANT INDUSTRIES
www. TyrantIndustriesPublishing.com

RICHARD MARSDEN
www.WorksofRichardMarsden.com

HENRY SNIDER
www.HenrySnider.com

Translation Commentary
Colin Hatcher

A little about my background: I have a language background of Latin, French, German and Spanish. I studied medieval English literature as an under-graduate in the late 1970s, developing from there a lifelong interest in medieval history and culture, especially the work of Chaucer. I researched and studied in the German language for my three years of post-graduate studies in the early 1980s. I have been researching and studying Fiore's Italian vernacular language for the past 17 years. I first began translating Fiore's Getty manuscript and his Pisani-Dossi facsimile in the year 2000. My motivation was simple: I found the available translations (of which there were very few) to be unsatisfactory and not very helpful in learning Fiore's art. Some were awkward literal translations that made little sense from a martial perspective, and they neither helped me to understand Fiore's martial system, nor did they help me to actually practice his Arte e Scientia d'Armizare (Art & Science of Armed Fighting). I believed at that time that I could do better, and I resolved to create a translation that was both accurate and that would be truly helpful to students trying to understand and practice the art. 16 years later I completed my first complete translation of the Getty in 2016 for the Wiktenauer Fiore E-Book project, and since then I have continued to evolve and improve the translation, the fruits of which you see here in this new 2017 translation.

Some brief comments to help you understand my translation approach:

1. I have translated all of Fiore's words into English. It is common practice in Fiore translations to leave many words and terms in the original language. I consider that a cop-out and have deliberately NOT done this, so that students can understand in English what Fiore is saying. I have however put lots of Fiore's Italian terms (such as guards, strikes and names for locks) in the original language in brackets next to my translations.

2. It's important to understand that the manuscript is written in verse (irregular/ loose rhyme or meter), perhaps for mnemonic purposes. To make it fit in verse (including a need to rhyme however loosely) Fiore has used many unusual expressions and many redundant words. In making my translation I have not attempted to create verse. I have given Fiore's unusual expressions their best equivalent translation and I have eliminated as much of the redundancy as I can (for example excessive over-use of the word "and").

3. My translation has been affected by my martial practice of Fiore. Where the translation makes no sense when the technique is actually performed (i.e. when the

translation does not help the student understand the technique), I have adapted the translation to match the actual technique. This process is necessarily interpretive. Sometimes for example the manuscript language is simply wrong (e.g. the text refers to the wrong prior drawing). Other times the drawing is wrong (e.g. a leg is drawn in front of a sword when the leg should be behind the sword). In some of these cases I have attempted in the translation to create some kind of concordance between words, drawing and actual practice.

4. I have deliberately attempted to make the translation conversational (oral) in tone (e.g. "I'm" rather than "I am"). This is both an accurate reflection of the tone of the text itself (the manuscript is written in Italian vernacular rather than in a literary language e.g. latin) and also makes for ease of reading and practical usage. You should note: the art would have been taught orally rather than from a book, so what the art sounds like when the translated text is spoken aloud is significant. Interestingly Fiore's manuscript was created during a time of (and therefore in defiance of) a strong classical latin literary revival in Italy. Fiore's vernacular language clearly indicates the obvious: that the work reflects a prosaic purpose – to record a martial system – rather than to create a work of high literary art.

5. In keeping with point 4. Above: I have 50 pages of linguistic footnotes that go with this translation (notes and research from over 16 years), but I have elected not to include them in this new publication. This reflects my own purpose: also prosaic! See below:

6. The purpose of this publication is to create a handbook of Fiore's art as depicted in the Getty manuscript, with an accurate readable translation for use in the field by HEMA students of Fiore. Don't treat this book as a coffee table book. Pick up a sword, and use this book!

Englishman Colin Hatcher, Esq. is by profession a trial attorney of 16 years, currently practicing law in Dallas, Texas, USA. He has been an active martial artist for 40 years and a martial arts instructor for over 25 years, during which time he has practiced many of the grappling arts (including wrestling, aikido, judo, Japanese jujitsu, and Brazilian jiu-jitsu), as well as kali/escrima (knife & stick fighting). From 1989 to 1998 he was an active and eventually full-time volunteer with community safety organization the International Alliance of Guardian Angels, rising to become International Director of training from 1992 to 1998, with responsibility for building and teaching that group's highly effective and reality tested "street-rules" martial arts programs.

Colin began his Historical European Martial Arts (HEMA) arts study and practice with the Schola Saint George in 1999 in California and was part of that school's first generation of students studying the martial art of Fiore dei Liberi (Arte e Scientia d'Armizare – the Art & Science of Armed Fighting. He rapidly became an instructor for the Schola Saint George and eventually served as its President between 2011-2014. He has organized, participated and fought in multiple medieval style tournaments, and has also taught HEMA classes at international symposia, including WMAW.

In 2014 Colin left the Schola Saint George to found his own HEMA school in Frisco, Texas, named Accademia del Leone (Academy of the Lion), where he continues to research, study and teach Fiore's Art & Science of Armed Fighting, including the arts of spear, longsword, dagger, and grappling.

Colin began studying Fiore's medieval Italian manuscripts, and their language, in 2000. He began his own primary translations of Fiore's Getty manuscript and the Pisani-Dossi manuscript in 2001-2002, eventually completing his Getty translation in 2016 for the Wiktenauer Fiore E-Book project. He has been researching for 17 years Fiore's language and the cultural and historical environment in which Fiore created his martial system.

ACCADEMIA DEL LEONE
https://www.facebook.com/groups/1504914743100636/

Format Commentary
Tracy Mellow

The inspiration for putting this project together began when I was studying the plays in the Getty manuscript (Ms. Ludwig XV 13), which is the most complete and concise of Fiore's manuscripts. As a visual learner, I was having difficulty in trying to decipher the plays when I had to jump between a copy of the manuscript, and a separate book or printout containing the translated text. it was frustrating and distracting. I really wanted the English translation and the manuscript to be in one book so I could more easily study the manuscript.

Since I founded, and run an historical fencing club, I wanted an English version of the manuscript that closely resembles the original to teach from, to get my students interested in learning from the source material, and to show to prospective students at demonstrations and other events to get them interested in learning more about the art.

That's where I got the idea of replacing the original Italian text with an English translation.

I also wanted the images labeled to easily locate certain plays, or Remedy Masters. The dagger section was difficult and time consuming to navigate since it is a long section. Trying to find the 8th Scholar (Student) of the 5th Dagger Remedy Master was time consuming. I got tired of counting crowns and garters to find the play I wanted. Fiore frequently refers to other plays in his text, so trying to locate the specific play he is referring to usually took some time. Labeling them makes it simple to navigate to the play he refers you to. I also liked the idea of studying the manuscript without a bunch of handwritten annotations from me labeling plays and images. I feel most connected to the art if I was studying the manuscript as closely to the original as possible without the distraction of handwritten annotations. The old way of studying the manuscript was not very efficient for a practicing martial artist to study from. I wanted to make the book easier to navigate.

The problem I had when beginning the first edition of the book was that I didn't have my own translation. I've done this art long enough that I can somewhat get the gist of some of the passages, but by no means had the linguistic skills needed to accurately translate the text myself. When I created the first version of this book in 2013 (Completed in 2014), I had contacted each of the contributors of the translated text from the Wiktenauer, a website that compiles all publicly available manuscripts, and asked permission to use their contributions. But some of the translations were somewhat dated, and came from different people, making the translation in the first edition not as smooth and polished as I would like it.

In March of 2017, I was approached by Richard Marsden and asked if I would create a new version of the book. This time, with an updated English translation written by Colin Hatcher. Colin spent over 12 years writing this translation to ensure it was translated as well as it could be. Colin was meticulous in his attention to detail in this translation, and is to date, the best full translation of the Getty I have seen. This book is the first time his full translation has been seen by the public.

This gave me the perfect opportunity to give the book a complete makeover. I was honored and happy to collaborate with them on this project to bring a complete study guide of the Getty manuscript that is indispensable to those who want to learn from the source material itself.

How this book differs from the original manuscript:

First, I replaced Fiore's original text with Colin Hatcher's English translation. Colin wrote this translation to where it could be understood by both those new to Armizare, and veterans of the art. There is not much in the way of technical jargon common with those who study the Historical European Martial Arts. This English translation will be great for those who are merely curious to get a glimpse into the mind of a fencing master. We decided to add some common Italian terminology where applicable. Those terms will be in brackets.

At the top of each passage, there is a series of numbers and letters (ie. 26v-a) That is the reference number used by the Wiktenauer to label each passage for easy reference. The numbers are the folio (page) number, which is on the bottom right corner of each page. The letter right after the number (r or v) refers whether it is the front or back of the page; r = Recto (Front) / v = Verso (back). The last letter refers to the location of the passage on the page. There are generally four images/passages per page (usually a, b, c or d), so the page is separated in quarters like this:

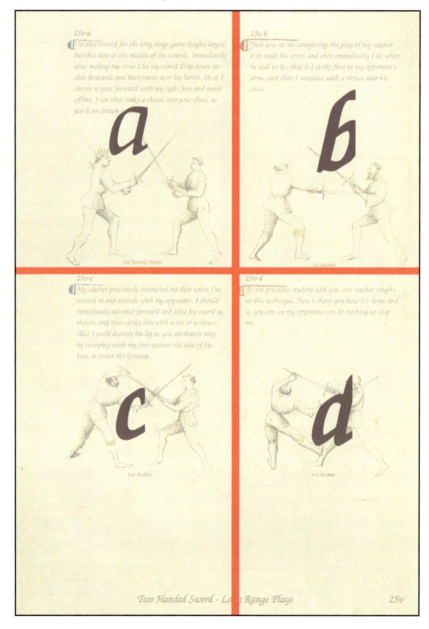

There are a few occasions where there are more than four images/passages per page. If the page has a passage at the top of the page, the reference number is denoted with a t. Other passages will be labeled in order they appear (ie. 9v-e), if more than four passages are on a page.

When you see a reference number within a passage, that means Fiore has mentioned a play from elsewhere in the manuscript, or is directly referring you to a play elsewhere within the manuscript. Colin has provided the reference number within the text to the play Fiore was referring to, making it much easier for you to find.

I labeled Remedy Masters in red, and Counter Masters in blue for quick, easy reference. Even the colors are significant. in the prologue, Fiore labels Remedy Master with a red paraph, and Counter Master with a blue paraph when introducing them. In addition to labeling the Fight Masters, Remedy Masters, Students, and Counter Masters, I also made it easier to find a counter to a play that is hidden in the text. I placed a blue * when a counter to a play is included in the text, but not the image, for easy reference. We wanted to make it easier for people to study the source material!

My annotations of the images are in small text. You will see some guards labeled in large red text on top of the image, and others in small red text below the image. That is because when Fiore labeled guards, he put them on top of the image. But there are many guards that are named in the text, but not labeled in the original manuscript. I felt it was important to label them, but wanted to keep this book as close to the original as possible, so instead of labeling them like Fiore did the others, I labeled them as an annotation below the image.

There are a few other annotations that are in small red text below an image besides Fight Masters (guards), and Remedy Masters. I labeled some important techniques that Fiore felt was important to name. For instance, in the dagger section, Fiore introduces a technique he calls the Middle Bind[ligadura mezana], and numerous times throughout the manuscript, Fiore states in the text of plays that you can put the opponent in the middle bind. Labeling that technique when introduced provides you with a quick reference to refer back to, to look at the image to see how to perform that technique.

I also made chapter headings at the beginning of each section, and at the bottom of each page I placed a page description for you to easily find a section.

After the prologue in the original manuscript, which is folio 1 and 2, there are a number of blank pages (Folio 3, 4, and 5) before the manuscript gets to the Grappling section on folio 6r. I have decided to leave these blank pages out since they serve no purpose. Folio 38 was misplaced in the original manuscript. It was placed at the end of the poleaxe section when rebound at some point in the past. It belongs in the dagger section, right after folio 14. So for this book, I placed it where it should be, but kept the folio number as given to it by the Getty museum. I hope you find this book to be an indispensable asset to your historical fencing studies. I know I do!

Photo courtesty Angel Uribe Photography

Tracy Mellow is from Visalia, California. He began his studies of Historical European Martial Arts in 1991 when he joined a full-contact armored sword fighting group. Tracy founded Iron Gate Swordfighting, an Historical European Martial Arts and Historical Fencing club in Visalia, and Fresno, California. Tracy is an Historical European Martial Arts Alliance certified instructor and teaches and specializes in Armizare, an Italian martial art created by 15th century fencing Master Fiore dei Liberi. Tracy has prior military experience and has had a career in law enforcement since 1998.

IRON GATE MARTIAL ARTS
http://irongatemartialarts.com/

The Flower of Battle
MS Ludwig XV 13

Fiore dei Liberi "The Flower Of Battle"
Ms. Ludwig XV 13

Table Of Contents

I the Friulian, born in Cividale D'Austria, am the son of Sir Benedetto of the noble order of the free knights of Premariacco, in the diocese of the Patriarchate of Aquileia. As a young man, I desired to learn armed fighting, including the art of fighting in the lists with spear, poleaxe, sword, dagger and unarmed grappling, on foot and on horseback, armored and unarmored. In addition I wanted to study how weapons were made, and the characteristics of each weapon for both offense and defense, particularly as they applied to mortal combat. I desired to learn the wondrous secrets of this art known only by very few men in this world, secrets that will give you mastery of attack and defense, and make you invincible, for victory comes easily to a man who has the skill and mastery described above. I learned these skills from many German and Italian masters and their senior students, in many provinces and many cities, and at great personal cost and expense. And by the grace of God I also acquired so much knowledge at the courts of noblemen, princes, dukes, marquises, counts, knights and squires, that increasingly I was myself asked to teach. My services were requested many times by noblemen, knights and their squires, who wanted me to teach them the art of armed combat both for fighting at the barrier and for mortal combat. And so I taught this art to many Italians and Germans and other noblemen who were obliged to fight at the barrier, as well as to numerous noblemen who did not actually compete.

Below are the names and a little of the history of some of the noblemen who've been my students, and who were obliged to fight at the barrier. The first of them was the noble and gallant knight Piero del Verde who fought Piero della Corona. Both were German, and the fight took place in Perugia. Next was the brave knight Niccolo Voriçilino, also a German, who was obliged to fight Niccolo Inghileso. The field of battle for this fight was Imola. Next was the well-known, valiant and gallant knight Galeazzo de Capitani da Grimello, known as da Mantova, who was obliged to fight the valiant knight Buçichardo de Fraca. The field of battle for this fight was Padua. Next was the valiant squire Lancillotto da Becharia de Pavia, who exchanged six strikes with a sharpened steel lance against the valiant German knight Baldassarro, in a fight that took place in the lists at Imola. Next was the valiant squire Gioanino da Bavo, from Milan, who, in the castle in Pavia, fought three passes with a sharpened steel lance, against the valiant German squire Sram. And then on foot he fought three passes with the axe, three with the sword and three with the dagger, in the presence of the very noble prince and lord the Duke of Milan, his lady the Duchess, and numerous other lords and ladies. Next was the cautious knight Sir Açço da Castell Barcho, who was obliged to fight one pass against Çuanne di Ordelaffii, and another pass against the valiant and good knight Sir Jacomo di Boson, at a location chosen by his eminence the Duke of Milan. I'm very proud of these and others whom I, Fiore, have taught, because I've been well rewarded, plus I earned the respect and the affection of my students as well as their families. I should tell you, by the way, that I always taught this art secretly, and so no one was present at my lessons except for the student and...

except for the student and occasionally a close relative of his.
So if anyone else was there by my grace or favor, they were
only allowed to watch after swearing a sacred oath of secrecy,
swearing by their faith not to reveal any of the techniques they
saw me, Master Fiore, demonstrate. More than anyone else I
was careful around other Masters of Arms and their students.
Some of these Masters who were envious of me challenged me
to fight with sharp edged and pointed swords wearing only a
padded jacket, and without any other armor except for a pair
of leather gloves. This happened because I refused to practice
with them or teach them anything about my art. I was
obliged to fight five times in this way. Five times, for my
honor, I had to fight in unfamiliar places without family or
friends to support me, with no one to trust but God, my art,
myself, and my sword. And by the grace of God, I acquitted
myself honorably and without injury to myself. I tell my
students who have to fight at the barrier that fighting at the
barrier is significantly less dangerous than fighting with sharp
swords wearing only padded jackets, because when you fight
with sharp swords, if you fail to cover one single strike you'll
likely die. On the other hand, if you fight at the barrier and
are well armored, you can still win the fight even if you take
a lot of hits. And here's another fact: at the barrier it's rare
that anyone dies from being hit. So as far as I'm concerned,
and as I explained above, I'd rather fight three times at the
barrier than one time in a duel with sharp swords. Next I
should add that a man may fight at the barrier well armored,
with a knowledge of the art of combat, and may have all the
advantages possible to have, but if he lacks courage he may as
well just go ahead and hang himself. Having said that, I can
say that by the grace of God none of my students have ever
lost at the barrier. On the contrary, they've always acquitted
themselves honorably. I should also point out that the noble
knights and squires to whom I showed my art of combat have
been very satisfied with my teaching, and have never wanted
any other instructor but me. In addition let me just say
that none of my students, including those mentioned above,
have ever owned a book about the art of combat, except for
Galeazzo da Mantova. And he put it well when he said that
without books you can't be either a good teacher or a good student of this art. And I can confirm that to be true: that this
art is so vast that there's no one in the world with a memory
large enough to be able to retain even a quarter of it. And
it should also be pointed out that a man who knows no more
than a quarter of the art has no right to call himself a Master.
Now I, Fiore, although I can read and write and draw, and
although I have books about this art, and have studied it for
40 years and more, don't myself claim to be a perfect Master
in this art, (although I am considered so by some of the fine
noblemen who've been my students). But I will say this: if,
instead of studying the Art of Armed Combat for 40 years,

I'd spent 40 years studying law, papal decrees and medicine,
then I'd be ranked a Doctor in all three of these disciplines.
And you should also know that in order to study the science
of arms I've endured great hardship, expended great effort and
incurred great expense, all so as to be a perfect student of this
art. It's my opinion that in this art there are few men in the
world who can really call themselves Masters, and it's my goal to
be remembered as one of them. To that end I've created this book
all about this martial art and the things related to it, including
weapons, their applications, and other aspects too. In doing this
I've followed the instructions given to me by the nobleman I
respect the most, who is greater in martial virtue than any other
I know, and who's more deserving of my book because of his
nobility than any other nobleman I could ever meet, namely, the
illustrious and most excellent noble, the all-powerful prince, Sir
NICOLO Marquis of Este,
Lord of the noble cities of Ferrara, Modena, Reggio, Parma and
others, to whom may God grant long life and future prosperity,
and victory over all of his enemies. AMEN.

I'm going to lay out this book according to
the preferences of my lord Marquis, and since
I'll be careful to leave nothing out, I'm sure
that my lord will appreciate it, due to his
great nobility and courtesy. I'll begin with
grappling, of which there are two types: grappling for fun, or
grappling in earnest, by which I mean mortal combat, where
you need to employ all the cunning, deceit and viciousness you
can muster. My focus is on mortal combat, and on showing
you step by step how to gain and defend against the most
common holds when you're fighting for your life. If you
wish to grapple you should first assess whether your opponent
is stronger or bigger than you, as well as whether he's much
younger or older than you. You should also note whether he
takes up any formal grappling guards. Make sure you consider
these things first. And whether you're stronger or weaker
than your opponent, be sure in either case that you know how
to use the grapples and binds against him, and how to defend
yourself from the grapples your opponent attacks you with.
If your opponent is not wearing armor, be sure to strike him
in the most vulnerable and dangerous places, for example the
eyes, the nose, the larynx, or the flanks. And whether fighting
in or out of armor, be sure that you employ grapples and binds
that flow naturally together. In addition, to be a good
grappler you need eight attributes, as follows: [1] strength,
[2] speed, [3] knowledge of superior holds; [4] knowledge of
how to break apart arms and legs; [5] knowledge of locks,
that is how to bind the arms of a man in such a way as to
render him powerless to defend himself and unable to escape;
[6] knowledge of how to strike to the most vulnerable points;
[7] knowledge of how to throw someone to the ground
without danger to yourself. And finally [8] knowledge of

how to dislocate arms and legs in various ways. As required, I'll address all of these things step by step through the text and the drawings in this book. Now that I've discussed some general rules for grappling, I'll discuss the grappling guards. There are a variety of grappling guards, some better than others. But there are four guards that are the best whether in or out of armor, although I advise you not to wait in any of them for too long, due to the rapid changes that take place when you're grappling. The first four Masters that you'll see with crowns on their heads will show you these four superior grappling guards. The first two are named the "Long Guard" [posta longa] and the "Boar's Tusk" [dente de cengiaro] and they can be used to counter each other. The second two are named the "Iron Gate" [porta di ferro] and the "Forward Guard" [posta frontale], and they can also be used to counter each other. From these four guards, whether you're in or out of armor, you can do all of the eight things I listed earlier, including holds, binds, dislocations, etc. You'll need to learn the guards of the Masters, how to distinguish the Students from the Players and the Players from the Masters, and finally the difference between the Remedy and the Counter. While a Counter will usually be presented after the Remedies are shown, sometimes there'll also be a special "Counter Remedy" that comes last of all. But let me make this clearer for you. The four primary guards or "positions" are easy to learn. Sometimes you'll take a guard and face your opponent without making contact, waiting to see what your opponent will do. These are called the positions or guards of the First Fight Master. And this First Fight Master wears a golden crown on his head, to signify that the guards he waits in provides him with a superior defense. And these four guards are best suited to apply the principles of my art of armed fighting, which is why the First Fight Master chooses to wait in these particular guards. Whether you call it a "position" or a "guard", you're referring to the same stance. As a "guard" it's used defensively, that is you use it to protect yourself and defend yourself from the strikes of your opponent. As a "position" it's used offensively, that is, you use it to position yourself in such a way in relation to your opponent so that you can attack him without danger to yourself. The next Master, who follows the first one who makes the four primary guards, comes to respond to these guards and to defend himself against an opponent who makes attacks that flow from the four primary guards shown earlier. And this Master also wears a crown, but he's named the Second Fight Master. He's also known as the Remedy Master, because he carefully selects his response to attacks flowing from the posts referred to above, and makes defenses that prevent him from getting struck. This Second Fight Master or Remedy Master has a group of students under him, who demonstrate the plays taught by the Remedy Master that follow the primary cover

or technique that he shows first as his remedy. And these students wear a golden garter under their knee, to identify themselves. These students will demonstrate all the remedies of the Remedy Master, until a Third Fight Master appears, who'll show the counters to the Remedy Master and his students. Because he can defeat the Remedy Master and his students, this third Master wears both the symbol of the Remedy Master – a golden crown · and the symbol of his students, · a golden garter below the knee. And this King is named the Third Fight Master, and he's also named the Counter Master, because he makes counters to the Remedy Master and his students. Finally let me tell you that in a few sections of this art we'll find a Fourth Master (or King) who can defeat the Third Fight Master (the Counter to the Remedy). And this King is named the Fourth Fight Master. He's also known as the Counter-counter Master. Be aware however that in this art few plays will ever go past the Third Fight Master, for to do so is very risky. But enough about this. As I've explained above, the grappling guards (shown by the First Fight Master), the remedies of the Second Fight Master (named the Remedy Master) and his students, the counter-remedies of the Third Fight Master (named the Counter Remedy, who counters the Second Fight Master and his students), and the Fourth Fight Master (named the Counter-counter Master), represent the foundation of my art of Grappling, whether you're in and out of armor. Furthermore, these four Fight Masters and their Students are also the foundation of the art of the Spear, which has its own guards, Masters and students. The same is true for the art of the Pole-axe, the One-handed Sword, the Two-handed Sword and the Dagger. In summary, these Fight Masters and their students, identified by their various insignia, although first presented here as governing principles of my art of Grappling [abrazare], are actually the foundation of my entire Art of Armed Fighting [arte d'armizare], whether you're on foot or on horseback, and whether you're in or out of armor. My purpose in structuring my art in this way is to make my system easier to learn, by using the same principles of the guards, the Master, the Remedy and the Counter throughout it, just as you see shown first in the section on grappling. And the text, the drawings and the plays will so clearly show you my art, that you'll have no trouble understanding it. Now let's move on to study the actual drawings of the plays and the accompanying text, and you'll see that I've spoken truly.

Blank

Blank

Blank

Grappling [Abrazare]

6r-a

I'm named the Long Guard [posta longa], and this is how I wait for you. In response to the first grapple that you attempt on me I'll place my raised right arm firmly behind your left arm, then I'll enter into the first grappling play [6v-a], and with that technique I'll force you to the ground. But if that technique looks like it'll fail me, then I'll transition into one of the other techniques that follow.

Long Guard [posta longa]

6r-b

I move against you using the Boar's Tusk [dente di zengiar], and with this move I'm sure to break your hold. From this guard I can transition to the Iron Gate [porta di ferro] guard, from where I'll be ready to force you to the ground. If my plan fails me because of your defense, then I'll seek other ways to hurt you, using locks, binds and dislocations, as you'll see shown in these drawings.

Boar's Tusk [dente di zingiar]

6r-c

I wait for you unmoving in the Iron Gate [porta di ferro], ready to perform my techniques with all of my skill. And this skill can be applied not only in the art of grappling, but also to critical parts of the art of the spear, the poleaxe, the sword and the dagger. I'm the Iron Gate, full of malice. Those who oppose me will inevitably end up in pain. And as for any of you who come against me, trying to apply techniques of your own, I'll force you to the ground.

Iron Gate [porta di ferro]

6r-d

I'm named the Forward Guard [posta frontale] and I'm used to get my hands on you. If I come against you in this guard, you might get your hands on me. But if you do I'll transition from this guard, and skillfully take you down to the Iron Gate. Then I'll make you suffer as if you had fallen into the depths of hell. I'll serve you so effectively with locks and dislocations that you'll quickly learn who is the superior fighter. And as long as my skill serves me, my techniques will never fail.

Forward Guard [posta frontale]

This is the first grappling play, and from every grappling guard you can arrive at this play, and in this grapple you proceed as follows: grip his right inside elbow with your left hand, and bring your right hand up behind and against his left elbow as shown here. Then quickly make the second grappling play [6v-b], that is, having gripped him like this, turn your body to the left, and as a result he either goes to the ground or his arm will be dislocated.

Remedy Master

As the First Grappling Remedy Master [6v-a] explained, you can be sure of putting this man to the ground, or else breaking or dislocating his left arm. *But if your opponent were to take his left hand off your shoulder in order to make a defense, **then you would quickly let go of your opponent's right arm, seize his left leg with your left hand, and place your right hand at his throat in order to throw him to the ground, as you see depicted in the Third Play that follows [6v-c].

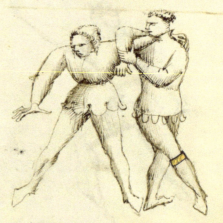

1st Student, *Counter, & **Counter-Counter

The student that came before me [6v-b] speaks truly that from his hold he'll either force his opponent to the ground or dislocate his left arm. But as he said, if the opponent takes away his left hand from your shoulder then you transition to the third play, as you see depicted here. Really the first play [6v-a] and the second play [6v-b] are one single play, where you force your opponent face down to the ground with a turn, whereas in this third play you throw the opponent to the ground onto his back.

2nd Student

This is the fourth grappling play, with which I can easily force my opponent to the ground. And if for any reason, I'm unable to force him to the ground like this, then I'll need to seek other plays and techniques and use other methods, as you'll see depicted below. You should know that these plays and techniques won't always work in every situation, so if you don't have a good hold, you should quickly seek one, so as not to let your opponent gain any advantage over you.

3rd Student

7r-a

This grip I make with my right hand at your throat will inflict pain upon you, and I'll force you to the ground with it. Also, let me tell you that if I seize you under your left knee with my left hand, I'll be even more certain of sending you crashing to the ground.

7r-b

I'm the counter of the fifth play [7r-a] shown previously. And let me tell you that if I push the elbow of my opponent's arm up upwards with my right hand as he seeks to harm me, I'll turn him in such a way that either I'll force him to the ground, as you see here depicted, or I'll gain a bind or a lock, and then I won't need to worry about his grappling moves.

4th Student

Counter Master to 4th & 6th Students

7r-c

From this hold I've gained, and by the way I hold you, I'll lift you off the ground with my strength and throw you down under my feet head first with your body following. And as far as I'm concerned, you won't be able to counter me.

7r-d

When I press my thumb under your ear you'll feel so much pain that either you'll drop to the ground, or I'll apply other binds and locks that'll be worse for you than if you were being tortured. *The counter you can make here is the sixth play made against the fifth play [7r-b], where you put your hand underneath your opponent's elbow and push up. That counter could certainly be done to me here.

5th Student

*6th Student & *Counter*

7v-a

You seized me from behind in order to throw me to the ground, but I turned like this. And if I fail here to throw you to the ground you'll have had a lucky escape. This play is a good finishing move, but unless it's done quickly, this remedy will fail.

7v-b

This is a play that involves a throw over the leg, which is not a very safe move in grappling, so if you want to make this leg throw work, you'll need to do it quickly and powerfully.

7th Student

8th Student

7v-c

This is a finishing move and it's a good technique to use to hold someone like this, because they can't defend themselves. *For the counter, the one who's being held should move as quickly as he can over to a wall or a post and throw himself backwards against it so that the man holding him cracks his head or his back against the wall or post.

7v-d

This student strikes his opponent with a knee to the groin to gain an advantage so as to throw him to the ground. *To make the counter, when your opponent comes in quickly to strike you in the groin with his knee, seize his right leg under the knee with your right hand, and throw him to the ground.

9th Student & *Counter

10th Student & *Counter

8r-a

If you seize me with both your arms underneath mine, I'll strike both my hands into your face. Even if you were well armored this would still make you let go. *The counter of this play is the one where you place your right hand under the left elbow of your opponent and push hard upwards [7r-b], so that you're able to free yourself.

11th Student & *Counter

8r-b

This shows how I make the counter to the thirteenth play [8r-a]. As you can see his hands have been removed from my face. And from this hold, if I fail to throw him to the ground I'll rightly earn your contempt.

Counter Master to 11th Student

8r-c

If you come to grips with both your arms underneath your opponent's, then you can still attack his face as you see depicted, especially if his face is not protected. You can also transition from here into the third grappling play [6v-c].

12th Student

8r-d

This is the counter to the fourteenth grappling play [8r-c], and to any other play where my opponent has his hands in my face while grappling with me. If his face is unprotected, I push my thumbs into his eyes. If his face is protected, I push up under his elbow [7r-b] and quickly move to a lock or a bind.

Counter Master to 12th Student

8v-a

¶ Observe how I hold you bound by your neck with a short staff. From here if I wish to throw you to the ground I'll have little trouble doing so, and if I choose to do worse to you I can continue to apply this strong bind, and you'll be unable to counter this play.

8v-b

¶ If you were well armored, then I'd rather make this play against you than the previous one [8v-a]. Now that I've caught you between your legs with the short staff, you're stuck riding it like a horse, but you won't be trapped like this long before I turn you upside down onto your back.

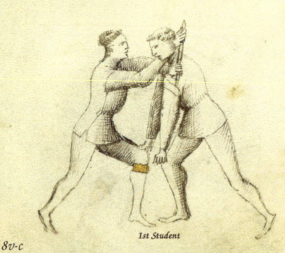

1st Student

2nd Student

8v-c

¶ I'm the student of the Eighth *Dagger Remedy Master [17r-c], who counters with his dagger just like this. So, it's in his honor that I make this cover with my short staff, and from here I can make all the plays of my teacher. This cover I've made with a short staff could also be done with a scarf, *and the counter to this move is the same counter shown by my Master [17r-d].

8v-d

¶ I've taken this remedy from the Sixth ** Remedy Master of the Dagger [16r-a], and I can defend myself armed only with this short staff. Having made this cover I rise to my feet, and I can then make all of the plays of my Master. I could defend myself in this way equally well with a hood or a piece of rope, *and the counter to this move is the same counter shown by my Master [16v-c].

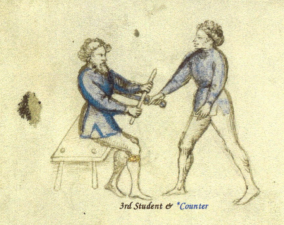

3rd Student & *Counter

4th Student & *Counter

* The manuscript mistakenly says it's the Sixth Dagger Remedey Master – it's actually the Eighth.

** The manuscript mistakenly says it's the Eighth Dagger Remedy Master – it's actually the Sixth.

Dagger [Daga]

9r-t
These five figures show the guards of the dagger. Some are good in armor; some are good without armor; some are good both armored and unarmored; and some are good armored but not unarmored. All five are displayed below.

9r-a
I'm Low Iron Gate single [tutta porta di ferro sempia]. I'm good armored and unarmored, because I can ward off an attack with or without moving to grapple, and I can play with or without a dagger when I make my covers.

9r-b
I'm Low Iron Gate doubled [tutta porta di ferro dopia]. I'm good armored and unarmored, but in all situations, I'm better armored than unarmored, and with a guard like this I can't use a dagger.

9r-c
I'm Middle Iron Gate doubled and crossed [meza porta di ferro dopia incrosada] [with dagger]. And I'm good in armor but not good out of armor, because I can't cover long. But I can cover above and below, from the right and from the left, and with or without a dagger.

Low Iron Gate doubled
[tutta porta di ferro dopia]

Low Iron Gate single
[tutta porta di ferro sempia]

9r-d
I'm Middle Iron Gate with dagger in hand. I'm doubled [mezana porta de ferro dopia cum la daga in mano], and I'm better and stronger than any of the others. I'm good armored and unarmored, and I can cover low and high on either side.

9r-e
I'm Low Iron Gate doubled with arms crossed [tutta porta di ferro dopia cum li brazi incrosadi]. I'm like a mighty fortress, and I'm especially strong in armor. But out of armor I'm not sufficient, because I can't cover long.

Middle Iron Gate doubled and crossed
[meza porta di ferro dopia incrosada]

Low Iron Gate Doubled and crossed
[tutta porta di ferro dopia incrosadi]

Middle Iron Gate doubled
[mezana porta de ferro dopia]

9v-a

¶ Everyone should be careful when facing the perilous dagger, and you should move quickly against it with your arms, hands and elbows, ¶ to do these five things, namely: ¶ take away the dagger; strike; dislocate the arms; bind the arms; and force your opponent to the ground. ¶ You should never fail to do one or the other of these five things. ¶ And may he who seeks to defend himself protect himself in this way.

9v-b

With falling strikes [fendente] you strike to the head and the body from the elbow up to the top of the head. But below the elbow you can't be sure you can make this strike without danger, so you should avoid striking any lower.

9v-c

¶ From the left side [parte reversa], you should strike reverse hand between the elbow and the temple of the head. These are called crosswise strikes. But these strikes from the left should not be attempted if you're still waiting to make cover against your opponent's attack.

9v-d

¶ From the right side [dritta parte], you can strike or cover as needed, and your target ranges from the elbows to the temple of the head. This strike is more safely made from the right side than the left side [9v-e].

9v-e

¶ The dagger that goes up through the middle [per mezo] towards the head strikes below the chest and never higher. And while striking you should at all times be making cover with your left hand.

9v-f

¶ I'm the noble weapon named the dagger and I play at very close range. He who understands my malice and my art will also gain a good understanding of many other weapons. I finish my fight so fiercely and quickly that there's no man who can stand against my method. If you watch my deeds of arms you'll see me make covers and thrusts as I move to grapple, and take away the dagger by dislocating and binding arms. Neither weapons nor armor will be of any use against me.

10r-a

I hold your dagger in my right hand, and I gained it through my skill, which is so advanced that if you draw a dagger on me, I'll take it from your hand. I also know how to strike to finish you, no matter what advantage you might have.

10r-b

I choose to symbolize my skill with the broken arms I carry. And I'm not lying when I tell you that I've broken and dislocated many arms in my life. And if you choose to go against my art you'll find me always ready to use that art against you.

10r-c

I'm the Master of the binding and dislocating of the arms of those who choose to oppose me. I'll cause great suffering with my techniques of binding and dislocating. And that's why I carry these keys to signify the level of my skill.

10r-d

You ask how I have this man pinned under my feet. Thousands have suffered this fate because of my grappling skills, and because no one can match my skills, I hold a victor's palm leaf in my right hand to signify my prowess.

10v-a

I'm the first master and I'm called Remedy, because I know how to defend so well that you can't harm me, whereas I on the contrary can strike you and hurt you. I can't make a better play against you than to make your dagger go to the ground, by turning my hand to the left.

10v-b

I'll turn my dagger around your arm. And because of this counter you won't be able to take the dagger from me. Also with this turn I'll drive my dagger into your chest for certain.

1st Remedy Master

Counter Master to *1st Remedy Master*

10v-c

I'll lock your arm in the middle bind [la mezana ligadura], and I'll do it in such a way that you won't be able to give me any trouble. And if from here I wish to put you to the ground I'll do so with little effort, and you'll have no chance of escaping.

10v-d

I make the counter to the play that came before me. You can see the kind of position that I've put him in. From here I'll break his arm or quickly throw him to the ground.

1st Student
Middle bind [la mezana figadura]

Counter Master to *1st Student*

11r-a

This is a good cover from which to take the dagger from your hand, and with this grip I'll be easily able to bind you. My method is so effective that if I place my right hand under your right knee, then I'll throw you to the ground.

11r-b

I make the counter to the play that came before me, and as a result you won't be able to throw me to the ground, nor take the dagger from me, nor bind me either. You'll have to let go, or you'll be quickly stabbed by my dagger.

2nd Student

Counter Master to 2nd Student

11r-c

This is a play with no counter, and if the student performs this technique as depicted, the opponent will inevitably be thrown to the ground and lose his dagger. And after the opponent has been thrown to the ground, the student can finish him in several different ways.

11r-d

This play is rarely used in the art of the dagger, yet it's an additional defense you should know. For after beating aside the attack in this way, the student can then strike with a counter to the ribs or the stomach.

3rd Student

4th Student

11v-a

I'm a counter to the First Dagger Remedy Master. Woe to he who tries to remedy with techniques that allow his left hand to be seized. And from this hold I can drive my dagger into his back.

11v-b

I'm also a counter of the First Dagger Remedy Master, and when his student grips me like this, I'll strike him, and make him let go. And if he tries to do other plays against me, I'll counter him immediately.

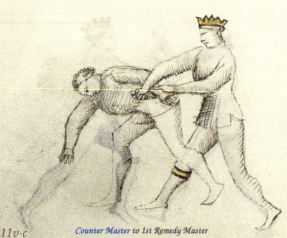

Counter Master to 1st Remedy Master

2nd Counter Master to 1st Remedy Master

11v-c

This flows from the counter referred to in the previous play [11v-b]. It also flows from the counter referred to two plays back [11v-a], where the Counter Remedy Master has trapped the hand of his opponent with his dagger, and where he told you that he can drive the dagger into his opponent's back. My play comes from that play, but where he says you drive the dagger into your opponent's back, I drive it into his chest. But this still flows from the previous play, even though I choose to finish it differently.

11v-d

I'm the student of the First Dagger Remedy Master. And with this grip I aim to take your dagger and bind your arm, and since I don't believe you know how to counter me, I'll do this to you immediately.

Counter-Counter Master to 2nd Counter Master

5th Student

12r-a

I counter you like this, so that you will neither take my dagger nor bind my arm, and so that my dagger and I will both remain at liberty. And then I can strike you when you let go of me in such a way that you'll have no defense.

12r-b

This cover is known to be much stronger and I make it so as to be able to obstruct you with various plays. And you can't overcome a strong cover like this, because two arms can easily oppose one arm.

Counter Master to 5th Student

12r-c

This is the counter to the cover that came before [12r-b], the one I told you was much stronger. Here I turn him with my left hand. Having turned him, I'll not fail to strike him.

12r-d

With this excellent grip that I have made on you, I'll not fail to break your arm over my left shoulder. And afterwards, since this play won't fail me, I can strike you with your own dagger.

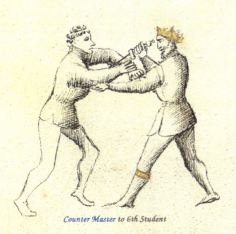

Counter Master to 6th Student

7th Student

12v-a

I make this counter to you who in the previous play intended to break my arm over your shoulder [12r-d]. I'll throw you hard to the ground to your death and you'll cause me no further injury.

12v-b

I'm in a good position to take the dagger from your hand, and to do it I push the point upwards, close to your elbow. You'll lose it, and then I'll quickly strike you with it. I took the dagger in this way because I couldn't bend your arm.

Counter Master to 7th Student

8th Student

12v-c

I make the counter to the play that came before [12v-b], to prevent you taking my dagger like that. I'll press my dagger into your hand, to make you let go, and with its cruel point I'll strike you for your trouble.

12v-d

You'll be driven into the ground like this, and you won't be able to make any defense or counter. And because of my skillful knowledge of this art, I'll quickly make the dagger that you hold in your hand go far from you.

Counter Master to 8th Student

9th Student

13r-a

You can't always do what you plan to do. I'm the counter of the student who came before [12v-d], and this counter will make him look very foolish, because in this way I'll make him let go of my leg. I'll also drive the dagger into his face to show him what a great fool he really is.

13r-b

I play with my arms crossed, and can make all the remedies that were previously shown. And if we were both armored, you couldn't make a better cover. No other crowned [Dagger] Remedy Master makes a stronger cover than I, for I can play both to the right and to the left, and I can cross from both underneath and from above.

Counter Master to 9th Student

2nd Remedy Master

13r-c

I counter the [Dagger] Remedy Master who made the cross before me [13r-b], so he won't be able to cause me any problems with his crossing. I'll give a push to his elbow to make him turn, and then I'll quickly strike him.

13r-d

I believe this very strong lock is fatal to anyone, because with it I can break your arm, throw you to the ground, or take your dagger. I can also hold you bound in the upper bind [la soprana ligadura]. And in addition to these four things, you'll be unable to get away.

Counter Master to 2nd Remedy Master

Student

13v-a

I know the counter to the previous play [13r-d]. And with this grip I'll counter all four of the plays he said he could do before. And as soon as he sees me, I'll throw him to the ground, for this grapple is strong and fierce.

Counter Master to Student

13v-b

Here begin the plays against reverse strikes made from the left, which have caused countless men to lose their lives. The plays of my students will follow, demonstrating how you make cover with your right hand. The play shown is easy to do, and I'll drive this man backwards into the ground as shown.

3rd Remedy Master

13v-c

With this play I'll drive you into the ground, and in armor I couldn't make a safer throw. But even if I'm not in armor, there's still nothing you can do, and even if you were strong and powerful, I'd still be able to do this to you.

1st Student

13v-d

You'll go to the ground and your arm will be dislocated by the skill of my crowned Master. And there's not one counter that you can do to me, for I hold you like this and I'll make you suffer greatly.

2nd Student

14r-a

¶ This is a lock that has no counter and no defense. In this way I can take your dagger, and I'll have no trouble binding or dislocating your arm. You won't be able to get away unless I release you, and I can destroy your arm at will.

14r-b

¶ You'll lose your dagger by the way I hold you. And after taking your dagger I can bind you, and make you suffer in the lower bind [ligadura di sotto], which is one of the key binds I'll use on you. Whoever is put into this lock can't escape, because of the great pain they'll be forced to endure.

3rd Student

4th Student

14r-c

¶ This is called the lower bind [ligadura di sotto], also known as the "strong key" [la chiave forte], and from this bind I can kill you, whether you're armored not, because from here I can strike you in all of your most vulnerable places. There is no escape from this bind, and if you're put into it, as shown in the drawing, there you'll remain, enduring endless suffering.

14r-d

¶ This is the counter to the Third Dagger Remedy Master [13v-b to 14r-c], who covers reverse strikes from the left. I've made this bind against him, and whether he's armored or unarmored, this bind is strong and secure. If I trap a man who's unarmored like this, I'll destroy and dislocate his hand, and the pain will be so great I'll force him to kneel at my feet. I can also strike him at will.

5th Student
Lower bind [ligadura di sotto]
or "strong key" [la chiave forte]

Counter Master to 3rd Remedy Master

14v-a

I'm the Fourth [Dagger Remedy] Master, and I play from this grip. From covers like this my students will hurt many people. And if I turn to my right without releasing your arm, I'll take your dagger as well as inflict great pain on you.

14v-b

This is an upper bind [ligadura soprana] that locks you up very well. I'll take your dagger from you and throw you to the ground. And I can also dislocate your arm. *If however you grip your right hand with your left hand, then you can counter me and make me let go of you.

4th Remedy Master

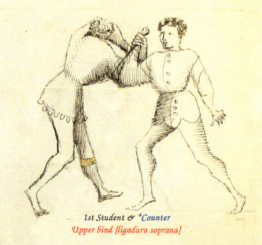

1st Student & *Counter
Upper bind [ligadura soprana]

14v-c

This is another upper bind [soprana ligadura] that's very powerful. And with this one I'm certain to throw you to the ground. And if I wish I can also dislocate your arm. *To counter me, you grip your right hand with your left hand. Then your grip will be strong and mine will be weak.

14v-d

After I made the cover of my Master, I put my left hand under your right elbow. And my right hand quickly gripped you under your knee in such a way that I could throw you to the ground, and there was no counter that you could do to me.

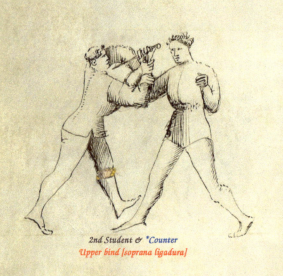

2nd Student & *Counter
Upper bind [soprana ligadura]

3rd Student

38r-a

With my right hand I'll make a horizontal turn to your dagger, pushing it round close to your arm that I am holding. Your dagger will be mine to control, and then I'll deal with you as you deserve.

38r-b

If I raise your dagger upwards close to your elbow, I'll keep it in my hand and strike you for certain. But I'll need to make this play very quickly, to make sure that you can't counter me with your left hand.

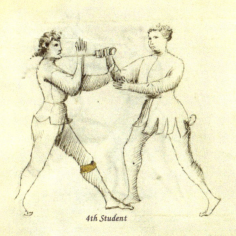

4th Student

5th Student

38r-c

I'm the Counter-remedy against the Fourth [Dagger] Remedy Master [14v-a], and I counter all his plays that came before me [14v-a to 14v-d, and 38r-a to 38r-b] And with one quick wrench like this I'll ruin this student's hand and his Master's too. And if they're well armored the ruin of their hands will be all the more certain.

38r-d

I'm the Fifth Dagger Remedy Master who defends against the collar grab as shown by this player. Before he can strike me with his dagger I destroy his arm like this, because the grip he has on me is actually to my advantage. I can do all of the covers, holds and binds of the other remedy masters and their students who came before me. And let me tell you this from experience: anyone who studies this art should be aware that you can't successfully defend against the collar grab unless you move quickly.

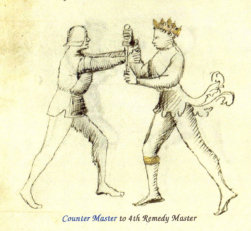

Counter Master to 4th Remedy Master

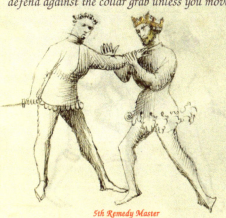

5th Remedy Master

*Folio 38 was misplaced in the manuscript. It was placed between the poleaxe and spear sections. It actually belongs after Folio 14

38v-a

This is another way to destroy the arm. And from this play I can move to other plays and holds. Also, if you're pinned by a spear then by making this strike against it you'll either unpin yourself or break off the haft from the spearhead.

38v-b

This is another way to make you let go, and is also a better method of breaking off the head of a spear. Also if I strike you hard in the wrist joint of the hand holding my collar, I'm certain to dislocate it unless you let go. *I wish also to tell you the counter. As the student strikes down with his arms to dislodge the player's hand, the player quickly withdraws his hand from the student's collar, and then quickly strikes the student in the chest with his dagger.

1st Student

2nd Student & *Counter

38v-c

This play will make you let go of me. And in addition, if I advance my right foot behind your left foot, you'll be thrown to the ground without fail. And if this play is not enough, I'll try others on your dagger, because my heart and my eyes are focused solely on taking away your dagger quickly and without delay.

38v-d

I'll throw you to the ground like this, before your dagger can get near me. And if your dagger comes down the center line to strike at me, I'll release my grip and deal with your dagger, so that you won't be able to injure me in any way. Then I'll make you suffer with my remedy plays.

3rd Student

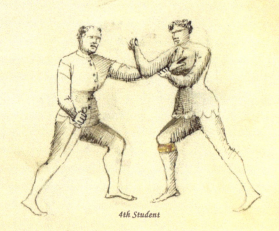

4th Student

15r-a

This player had me grabbed by the collar, but before he could strike me with his dagger I quickly seized his left hand with my hands and pulled his arm over my shoulder in order to dislocate it, and then I completely dislocated it. But note: this play is safer to do in armor than unarmored.

15r-b

I'll hurl you to the ground like this without fail, and I'll surely take your dagger. If you're armored that may help you, since I'll be aiming to take your life with your own dagger. But even if you're armored, this art won't fail me. If you're unarmored and very quick, other plays can be made besides this one.

5th Student

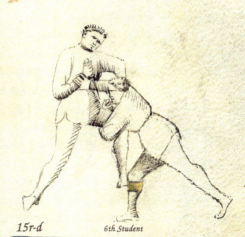

6th Student

15r-c

This cover is very good armored and unarmored, and against any strong man this cover is good for covering an attack from below as well as from above. From this play you can enter into the middle bind [ligadura mezana] as shown in the third play of the First Dagger Remedy Master [10v-c]. And if the cover is made in response to an attack from below, the student will put the player into a lower bind [ligadura de sotto] also known as "the strong key" [la chiave forte], as shown in the sixth play of the Third [Dagger] Remedy Master who plays against strikes from the left [14r-c].

15r-d

If I can turn your arm I'll be certain to put you into the lower bind [ligadura de sotto] or "strong key" [chiave forte]. However, I'll be able to do this more safely if I'm armored. I could also do something else against you: if I grip your left hand firmly and seize you under your left knee with my right hand, then I'll have the strength to put you to the ground.

7th Student

8th Student

15v-a

With arms crossed I fearlessly wait for you. I don't care whether you come at me from above or below, because either way you'll end up in a bind. You'll be locked either in the middle bind [ligadura mezana] or the lower bind [la sottana]. If I wished to make the plays of the Fourth Dagger Remedy Master [14v-a to 14v-d, and 38r-a to 38r-b], I'd cause you great harm with these plays, and I'll have no difficulty taking your dagger.

15v-b

This grip is sufficient to prevent you being able to touch me with your dagger. And from here I can do the play that comes after me [15v-c]. And I could also certainly do other plays to you. I disregard the other plays for now, however, because this one is good for me and very fast.

9th Student

10th Student

15v-c

This is the play referred to by the student who came before me, and I take away this dagger as he indicated. To disarm him I push his dagger downwards and to the right as described above. And then by making a turn with his dagger I thrust the point into his chest without fail.

15v-d

To prevent this student from dislocating my arm, I pull it towards me and bend it. And the farther I pull it towards me and bend it, the better, because in this way I make the counter to the [Fifth] Remedy Master in the close play of the dagger.

11th Student

Counter Master to 5th Remedy Master

16r-a

I am the Sixth [Dagger Remedy] Master, and let me tell you that this cover is good either in armor or out of armor. With this cover I can cover attacks from all directions and enter into all of the holds and binds, and strike to finish, as the students who follow me will show. Each of my students will make this cover, and then they'll make the plays shown after, according to their skill.

16r-b

I made the cover of my Master, the Sixth [Dagger Remedy] Master who preceded me, and as soon as I've made this grip I'll be able to strike you. Because I position my left hand in this way, I won't fail to take away your dagger. I can also put you in the middle bind [ligadura mezana], which is the third play of the First Dagger Remedy Master [10v-c]. I could also make other plays against you without abandoning my dagger.

6th Remedy Master

1st Student

16r-c

I've made this half turn from the cover of the Sixth Master and I've quickly positioned myself to strike you. And even if you were armored I'd care little, for in that case I'd thrust this dagger in your face. However, as you can see, in this case I've thrust it into your chest because you're unarmored and you aren't familiar with close range play [zogo stretto].

16r-d

I haven't abandoned the cover of my Master, the Sixth [Dagger Remedy] Master. I turn my left arm over your right, and moving my right foot at the same time as my left arm I turn myself to the outside. You're now partly bound, and you'll have to admit that now you'll quickly lose your dagger. I make this play so quickly that I've no concern for, nor fear of, any counter from you.

2nd Student

3rd Student

After making my Master's cover, I made this grip, and now I can strike you whether you're in or out of armor. I can also put you into the upper bind [ligadura soprana] of the first student of the Fourth Dagger Remedy Master [14v-b].

Without abandoning the cover of the Sixth [Dagger Remedy] Master, I make this turn [with my dagger]. Your right hand will lose the dagger, and after you've been reversed, my dagger will quickly strike you, and you'll lose your dagger. I can also make a turn with my left arm and make you suffer in the lower bind [la sotana ligadura].

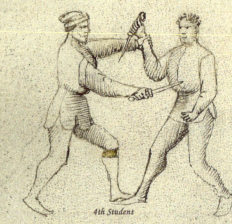

4th Student

5th Student

I make the counter-remedy of the Sixth King [Dagger Remedy Master], turning your body with an elbow push, and in this way I can strike you, because with this quick elbow push, I'll be able to defend against many close-range plays [zoghi stretti]. This is a particularly good counter-remedy to all of the holds of the close-range game.

Although I'm placed after the counter-remedy to the Sixth Master [16v-c], I should logically be placed before him, because I'm a student of the Sixth [Dagger Remedy] Master and my play belongs to him. This play makes more sense in armor than unarmored, because if he is armored I can strike him in the hand where he cannot fully protect himself; whereas if he's unarmored, I would aim to strike him in the face or in the chest, or in some other vulnerable place.

Counter Master to 6th Remedy Master

6th Student

19

17r-a

I'm the Seventh [Dagger Remedy] Master and I play with my arms crossed. This cover is better made in armor than unarmored. The plays that I can do from this cover are the plays that came before me, especially the middle bind [ligadura mezana] which is the third play of the First Dagger Remedy Master [10v-c]. I can also turn you by pushing your right elbow with my left hand, and I can quickly strike you in the head or in the shoulder. This cover is better for binding than any other cover, and is a very strong cover to make against the dagger.

17r-b

This is the counter remedy to the plays of the Seventh [Dagger Remedy] Master who came before me. Let me explain that with the push that I make to his right elbow, this counter-remedy is good against all close-range plays [zogo stretto] of the dagger, the poleaxe, and the sword, whether in armor or unarmored. Once I've pushed his elbow I should quickly strike him in the shoulder.

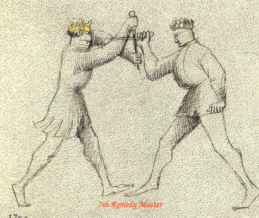

7th Remedy Master

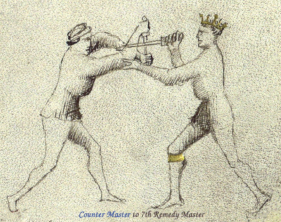

Counter Master to 7th Remedy Master

17r-c

I'm the Eighth [Dagger Remedy] Master and I cross with my dagger. This cover is good both in armor or unarmored. Some of my plays are shown before me, and some are shown after me. In the play that is shown before me, three plays back, the player was struck in his hand with the point of his opponent's dagger [16v-d]. Similarly, in this play I could strike downwards to his hand just as in the earlier play I struck upwards to his hand. Also, I could seize his hand at the wrist with my left hand, and then strike him hard with my right hand, as you will see demonstrated by the ninth student of the Ninth [Dagger Remedy] Master, who strikes the player in the chest [18v-c]. Also, I could do the last play that follows after, where I drop my own dagger and take his [18v-d].

17r-d

I'm the counter-remedy to the Eighth [Dagger Remedy] Master that preceded me, and to all of his students. If I extend my left hand to his [right] elbow, I can push it so strongly that I can strike him when he's turned. Also, as I make him turn I can throw my arm around his neck and hurt him in a variety of ways.

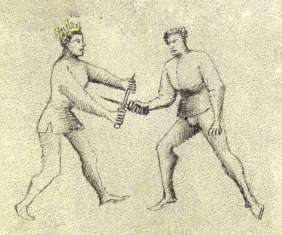

8th Remedy Master

Counter Master to 8th Remedy Master

17v-a

This guard makes a strong cover whether you're armored or unarmored. It's a good cover because from it you can quickly put your opponent into a lower bind [ligadura de sotto] or "strong key" [chiave forte]. This is what's shown in the sixth play of the Third [Dagger Remedy] Master [14r-c] who defends against the reverse hand strike and who uses his left arm to bind the player's right arm.

17v-b

This cover I make with my arms crossed is good whether you're armored or unarmored. My play puts my opponent into the lower bind [ligadura di sotto], which is also called the "strong key" [chiave forte]. That's the one the student who preceded me told you about, namely the sixth play of the Third [Dagger Remedy] Master who defends with his right hand against the reverse hand strike from the left [14r-c]. This play is made similarly to the play that immediately preceded me [17v-a], but it begins in a slightly different way. *Our counter—remedy again is the elbow push.

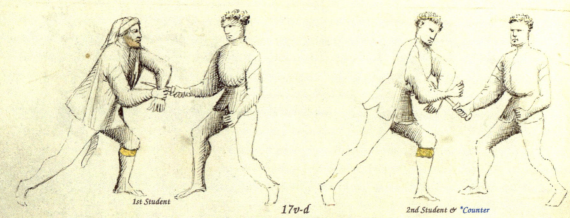

1st Student   2nd Student & *Counter

17v-c

I'm the Ninth King [Dagger Remedy Master] and I no longer have a dagger. The grip I make against a low attack is similar to the grip made by the Fourth King [Dagger Remedy Master] [14v-a], only this one is made against a low attack instead of a high attack, and my plays aren't the same as his. This grip is good whether you're armored or unarmored, and you can make many good strong plays from it, as shown below. Whether you're in armor or unarmored there's no doubt of the effectiveness of these plays.

17v-d

I've followed on from the grip of the Ninth [Dagger Remedy] Master [17v-c]. Taking my right hand from the grip, I seize your dagger as shown and rotate it upwards close to your elbow. I'll then thrust the point strongly into your face, or I'll deal with you as the next student will demonstrate.

9th Remedy Master

1st Student

20

18r-a

I complete the play of the student who came before me [17v-d], and from his grip this is how he should finish his play. Other students will make different plays from his grip. Watch those who follow, and you will see their techniques.

18r-b

My Master's grip has already been demonstrated. Here my right hand leaves that grip. And if I grip you under your elbow, I can dislocate your arm. Also from this grip I can put you into the bind known as the "strong key" [chiave forte], which is one the third King and [Dagger Remedy] Master showed in his plays. In his sixth play [14r-c] he shows you how this one is done.

2nd Student

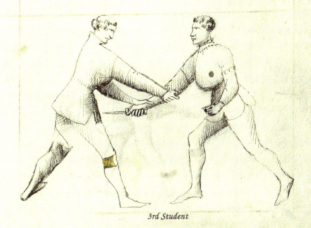

3rd Student

18r-c

I've arrived at this position from the grip of my Master [Ninth Dagger Remedy Master], but I don't remain in this grip but instead move into the lower bind [ligadura de sotto] known as the "strong key" [chiave forte]. I can do this without difficulty, and I can then easily take your dagger.

18r-d

I haven't abandoned the grip of my Master [the Ninth Dagger Remedy Master], but I've quickly entered under his right arm, to dislocate it with this grip. I can do this whether he's wearing armor or not, and once I have him held from behind and in my power, I'll show him no mercy as I hurt him.

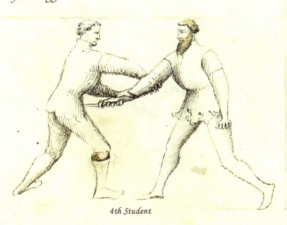

4th Student

5th Student

18v-a

¶ I didn't abandon the grip of my Master [the Ninth Dagger Remedy Master] and my opponent saw that he couldn't break my grip on his arm. As he pressed downwards towards the ground with his dagger, I quickly reached through his legs from behind and grabbed his right hand with my left hand. Once I had a good grip on his hand, I stepped behind him, and as you can see in the picture, he can't dismount his own arm without falling. I can now also do the play that follows me: if I let go of the dagger with my right hand, and grab his foot I'll send him crashing to the ground, and I can't fail to take his dagger.

18v-b

¶ The student who preceded me [18v-a] performed the first part of this play, and I complete it by driving him into the ground, as has already been explained. Although this play is not commonly performed in this art, I wish to show you that I have a complete knowledge of it.

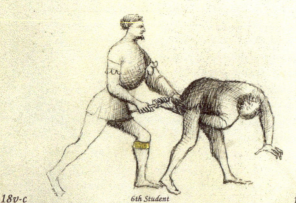

6th Student

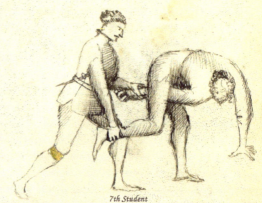

7th Student

18v-c

¶ I made the cover of my Master [the Ninth Dagger Remedy Master] and then I quickly gripped him like this with my left hand. Then I drew my dagger and thrust it into his chest. If I don't have time to draw my dagger, I'll make the play that follows me.

18v-d

¶ With this play I complete the play of the student who preceded me [18v-c], who left his [sheathed] dagger where it was and instead decided to take your live dagger. I've already explained how this play is performed.

¶ *The Counter-remedy to this Ninth [Dagger Remedy] Master's play is as follows: when the opponent with his left hand has seized your right hand that holds the dagger, then you should quickly seize your dagger near the point and strongly draw or pull it back towards you, so that he has to let go of it, or alternately you press the dagger point into his elbow to make him think twice.

8th Student

9th Student & *Counter

19r-a

Here begin sword against dagger plays, and you'll have a significant advantage if you know how to do these. This Master waits in a guard named Boar's Tusk [dente di zenghiaro], a guard that protects me from both cuts and thrusts. As I beat aside my opponent's sword, I pass backwards with my right foot, for I know the Close Range Game [lo zogo stretto] so well it cannot fail me. Attack me one by one as you wish. None of you will escape as I destroy each of you with this turn of my dagger.

19r-b

I've made the cover against the thrust that my Master showed you [19r-a], and now I quickly strike my opponent in the face or the chest. With dagger versus sword you should always aim to close with your opponent. Here, since I'm at close range I can strike you effectively, and whether you like it or not, you'll have to endure it.

1st Remedy Master

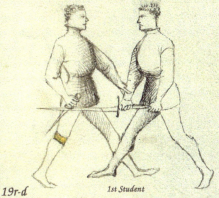

1st Student

19r-c

If the attacker in the previous picture [19r-b] had known how to defend himself, he would've reached across with his left hand and seized the opponent behind his left elbow, turning him in the manner shown here. Then he would've had no need of a counter to the remedy of the Dagger Master.

19r-d

If the Dagger Master is attacked with a falling strike to the head, he steps forward quickly, making the cover shown, turns his opponent by pushing his elbow, and then immediately strikes him. He can also bind the opponent's sword with his arm, as shown in the fourth play of the sword in one hand [20v-c & 20v-d]. You'll also find this middle bind [ligadura mezana] shown in the third play of the dagger [10v-c], which is made a hands-breadth from the face.

Counter Master to 1st Student

2nd Student

Sword vs Dagger

19v-a

This is one way to defeat the dagger in dagger against sword. The man with the dagger grabs the man with the sword by the collar and warns: "I'll strike you with my dagger before you can draw your sword from its scabbard." The man with the sword says "Try and strike me then, for I'm ready." And as the man with the dagger attacks, the man with the sword responds in the manner shown in the next picture.

19v-b

When the man with the dagger raises his arm to strike me, I immediately press the sheath of my sword against his dagger arm in such a way that his arm is jammed. I then quickly draw my sword, and I can strike him before he has a chance to even touch me with his dagger. I could also take the dagger from his hand using the method of the First Dagger Remedy Master [10v-a], or I could put him into the middle bind [ligadura mezana], using the third play of the First Dagger Remedy Master [10v-c].

1st Remedy Master

Student

19v-c

Here's another way for the sword to defeat the dagger. In this one I hold my sword with its point on the ground, as you see drawn here, and I say to the man with the dagger, who's grabbed me by the collar: "Go ahead and attack me with your dagger from this position. And when you try I'll strike against your arm with my sword still in the scabbard, then I'll draw my sword as I pass backwards with my right foot, and in this way I'll be able to strike you with my sword before you're able to strike me with your dagger."

19v-d

This is a similar defense to the one shown before, although it's done slightly differently. As the man with dagger raises his arm to strike, I quickly raise my sheathed sword up under his dagger, aiming the point of my sheathed sword into his face, while at the same time passing back with my lead foot. From here I can strike him as you see drawn in the next picture.

3rd Remedy Master

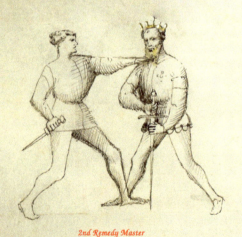

2nd Remedy Master

20r-a

This is the continuation of the play of the Master who made the preceding defense [19v-d], and I'm performing it exactly as he said to do it. As you can plainly see, you'll give me no trouble with your dagger.

Student

20r-c

Here are three opponents who all want to kill this Master. The first aims to kill him with a thrust. The second intends a cut. The third will throw his sword at the Master like a spear. If the Master can perform a mighty deed and avoid being killed, then God will have indeed blessed him with great skill.

One Handed Sword [Spada un Mani]

20r-d

You're all cowards and know little of this art. You're all just words without any deeds. I challenge you to come at me one after another, if you dare, and even if there are a hundred of you, I'll destroy all of you from this powerful guard. I'll advance my front foot a little off the line, and with my left foot I'll step crosswise, and as I do so I'll cross your swords, beating them aside and leaving you unprotected. I'll then strike you without fail. And even if you throw your spear or sword at me, I'll beat them all aside in the same manner I described above, s tepping off the line as you will see me demonstrate in the plays that follow, and which you would do well to study. And even though I'm only holding my sword in one hand, I can still perform all of my art, as you will see demonstrated in this book.

Remedy Master

I've done what my teacher told me to do. That is to say, I stepped off the line making a strong cover. Having rendered my opponent unprotected I now easily place a thrust into his face. And with my left hand I'll demonstrate that I can take his sword, and send it to the ground.

I've rendered you completely unprotected, and now I'll easily strike you in the head. If I choose to pass forward with my rear foot, I can perform close range techniques against you, such as locks, dislocations and grapples.

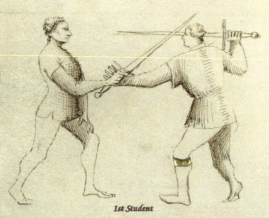

1st Student

2nd Student

From this position I can easily strike or stab you. And if I advance my front foot forward, I can lock you in the middle bind [ligadura mezana], as shown in the third play of the first Remedy Master of the dagger [10v-c]. Alternately I can do the play shown next, and bind and strike you as shown there.

Here both your sword and your arm are effectively trapped, and you won't be able to escape before I strike you as described, because you've shown you have no idea what I'm doing in this play.

3rd Student

4th Student

21r-a

¶ Here I can easily strike you while taking your sword, and by rotating it in your hand I'll make you drop it, as the only way to prevent yourself being thrown to the ground.

21r-b

¶ Here I can strike you from the front, but this isn't enough. By gripping your elbow I make you turn away, then I wrap my sword around your neck from behind, and you'll have no defense to this.

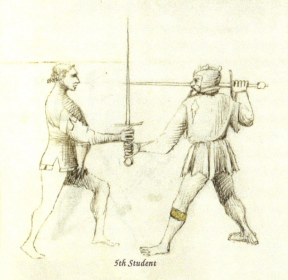

5th Student

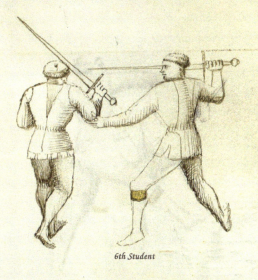

6th Student

21r-c

¶ In the previous drawing, I told you I'd turn you and then quickly wrap my sword around your neck, as shown here. Now if I fail to cut your throat, then I'm a pathetic fool.

21r-d

¶ You aimed a thrust at me and I beat it to the ground. Do you see how you're now unprotected and can be struck? I can also turn you and do you even more harm, by striking you from behind.

7th Student

8th Student

21v-a

Because I turned you by pushing your elbow, I've quickly come to this position, and from here I can throw you to the ground, where you'll no longer be able to fight me or anyone else.

9th Student

21v-b

This opponent struck at my head, and I beat his sword to the ground, coming to the position you see shown here. Now after forcing him to turn away, I'll aggressively wrap my sword around his neck.

10th Student

21v-c

This is a play where, if you wish to make this kind of thrust, you should be armored. If your opponent strikes at you with a thrust or a cut, you first make your cover, then quickly counter attack as shown.

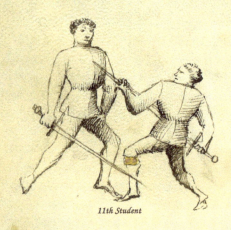

11th Student

One Handed Sword

Two Handed Sword [Spada dui Mani]

22r-a

We're two guards that are similar to each other, and yet each one's a counter to the other. And for all other guards in this art, guards that are similar are counters to each other, with the exception of the guards that stand ready to thrust—the Long Guard [posta lunga], the Short Guard [posta breve] and the Middle Iron Gate [meza porta di ferro]. For when it's thrust against thrust the weapon with the longer reach will strike first. Whatever one of these guards can do so can the other. From each guard you can make a fixed turn [volta stabile] or a half turn [meza volta]. A fixed turn is when without actually stepping you can play to the front and then to the rear on the same side. A half turn is when you make a step forwards or backwards and can switch sides to play on the other side from a forwards or backwards position. A full turn [tutta volta] is when you circle one foot around the other, one remaining where it is while the other rotates around it. Furthermore, you should know that the sword can make the same three movements, namely fixed turn, half turn and full turn. Both of these guards drawn below are named the Guard of the Lady [posta di donna]. Also, there are four types of movement in this art: passing forwards [passare], passing backwards [tornare], advancing [accressere], and withdrawing [discresse].

Guard of the Lady [posta di donna]

Guard of the Lady [posta di donna]

22r-c

We're six guards and each of us is different from the other, and I'm the first to speak of my purpose. My method is to throw my sword. The other guards follow after me. I believe they will tell you themselves about their particular virtues.

22r-d

I'm a good guard in or out of armor, and against a spear or a sword thrown from the hand, I'm confident I won't be harmed, because I know how to beat them aside and thus evade them.

Unnamed Guard - Throwing

Unnamed Guard - Deflection

22v-a

I'm the guard to use if you want to extend a long thrust, because my grip on the sword increases its reach. I'm good to use against you if you and I are armored, because I can make a quick thrust to the front which won't miss you.

22v-b

I'm a good guard against sword, axe and dagger if I'm armored, because I grip the sword with my left hand at the middle. This is particularly useful against the dagger, which can do more harm to me at close range than the other weapons.

Unnamed Guard - Long thrust

Unnamed Guard - Half sword

22v-c

I'm named the Guard [guardia] or Position [posta] of the Lady [di donna], and I'm different from the four sword guards that came before me, even though they're themselves different from each other. Although the next guard that opposes me seems to be my guard too, you'll note that I'm not using my sword reversed as a poleaxe, whereas that's how he's using his.

22v-d

This sword is being used as both a sword and a poleaxe. And its great force can stop any attack from a lighter weapon. This guard is also the High Guard of the Lady [posta de donna la soprana], who with her skill can fool the other guards, because you'll think she's going to attack you with a strike, but instead she'll attack you with a thrust. All I have to do is raise my arms above my head, and I can then quickly launch a thrust at you.

Guard of the Lady [posta di donna]

High Guard of the Lady [posta de donna lo soprana]

23r-a

We're the falling blows [colpi fendenti]. In this art our method is to cut with precision from the teeth down to the knee. And we can easily end up in any of the low guards. We're highly effective in breaking the other guards, and with each blow we make we leave a trail of blood. We falling blows strike fast, after which we return to our guard back the way we came.

Falling Blows [Colpi Fendenti]

23r-b

We're the rising blows [colpi sottani], and we go from the knee to the middle of the forehead, following the same path that the falling blows follow. And we return down the same path as we ascend, unless we choose to remain high in the Long Guard [posta longa].

Rising Blows [Colpi Sottani]

23r-c

We're the crosswise blows [colpi mezani], and we're so-called because we go crosswise through the middle of the path of both the falling blows and the rising blows. We strike with the true edge of the sword from the right, and with the false edge of the sword from the left, and our path could be anywhere between the knee and the head.

Crosswise Blows [Colpi Mezani]

23r-d

We're the cruel and deadly thrusts [punte]. Our target lies on the body's center line, and we can strike anywhere between the groin and the forehead. And we thrusts can be made in five ways: two of us can be made from high guards, one from each side [the two window guards], and two can be made from low guards, also one from each side [Low Iron Gate & Boar's Tusk]. The fifth one comes from a center line guard, and can be made from Middle Iron Gate [meza porta di ferro], the Long Guard [posta lunga], or the Short Guard [posta breve].

Thrusts [Le Punte]

Here begin the guards of the two handed sword [spada a doy man], and there are twelve of them. The first is Low Iron Gate, which is a very s trong guard, and a good guard in which to wait for an attack by every kind of hand-held weapon, whatever its length, as long as you have a good sword that is not too long. If you cover from this guard while making a passing step you'll transition to close range [le strette]. Or you can exchange thrusts, striking home with yours. Or, as you step, you can beat the opponent's thrust to the ground. This guard can cover attacks from all angles.

Iron Gate - powerful
[porta di ferro - pulsativa]

This is the Guard of the Lady [posta di donna], from which you can make all seven of the sword's strikes and cover them too. From this guard you can break the other guards with the strong blows you can make, and you can also quickly exchange thrusts. If you advance your front foot offline, then pass diagonally with your rear foot, this will take you to a position where your opponent is unprotected, and you'll then be able to quickly strike him.

Right side Guard of the Lady - powerful
[posta de donna destraza - pulsativa]

This is the Window Guard who is always quick, skillful and deceptive. It's a master at covering and striking. It threatens all opposing guards, whether high guards or low guards. It moves quickly from this guard to other guards to confuse its opponent, and it is a very good guard from which to make powerful thrusts, break the opponent's thrust or exchange points.

Window Guard - fluid
[posta de finestra - instabile]

This is the left side Guard of the Lady [posta di donna], and it's always quick to cover or strike. It generates powerful blows and easily breaks the thrust, driving it to the ground. Also, because of its skill in entering, you can quickly transition from it to the Close Range Game [lo zogho stretto], a game this guard is very familiar with.

Left side Guard of the Lady - powerful
[posta di donna sinestra - pulsativa]

24r-a

This guard is the Long Guard [posta longa], which is very deceptive. It's skilled in probing the guards to see if it can mislead its opponent. If it needs to strike the opponent with a thrust, it's well-suited to do so. As for the opponent's blows, it knows how to avoid them and then strike back with blows of its own. This guard employs deception more than any other guard.

24r-b

This is Middle Iron Gate [mezzana porta di ferro], so-called because it holds the center line and is a strong guard. But you don't want to hold your sword too far forward. It throws powerful thrusts and strongly strikes its opponents' swords upwards, then it returns to its guard with a falling blow to the head or arms. It's called Iron Gate because it's a strong guard, and it's dangerous to try and break it, because to do it you have to move into close range [ale strette].

The Long Guard - fluid
[posta longa - instabile]

Middle Iron Gate - fixed
[porta di ferro mezana - stabile]

24r-c

This is the Short Guard [posta breve] that's more effective with a longer sword. It's a deceptive guard but it's risky to wait in. It's constantly moving, trying to see if it can enter with a thrust and a step against the opponent. This guard is more effective in armor than unarmored.

24r-d

This is the Boar's Tusk [dente di zenghiaro], because it strikes the way the wild boar strikes. Sometimes it makes powerful rising thrusts up into the face, without stepping forward, and it returns along the same path with a falling blow to the arms. Other times as it thrusts the point of the sword high into the face, it advances the front foot forwards, then returns to its guard with a falling strike to the head or the arms. Then it quickly launches another thrust with another advance of the front foot. This guard can mount a good defense against the Close Range Game [lo zogo stretto].

The Short Guard - fixed
[posta breve - stabile]

The Boar's Tusk - fixed
[dente di cenghiaro - stabile]

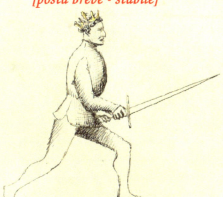

24v-a

This is the Long Tail Guard [posta di coda longa] that extends behind you down to the ground. It can attack with a thrust, and can also move forwards to cover and strike. And if it passes forward while striking downwards it can easily enter the Close Range Game [lo zogo stretto]. This is a good guard to wait in, because you can quickly transition from it into other guards.

24v-b

This is the Two Horned Guard, which is held so strongly locked in position that its point cannot be moved off the center line. This guard can do all of the things that the Long Guard [posta longa], the Window Guard [posta di fenestra] and the Forward Guard [posta frontale] can do.

Long Tail Guard - fixed
[posta di choda longa - stabile]

Two-horned Guard - fluid
[posta di bicorno - instable]

24v-c

This is the Forward Guard [posta frontale] called by some instructors the Crown Guard [posta di corona]. It's a very good guard for crossing swords, and is also very good against thrusts. If it's attacked with a high thrust, it crosses swords while stepping off line [fuora di strada]. If it's attacked with a low thrust, it also steps offline [fuor di strada], but this time it drives the opponent's sword to the ground. It can also do other things. For example, in response to a thrust it can pass backwards [torna] with the front foot [lo pe' indredo *] and respond with a falling strike to the head or arms, ending in the Boar's Tusk [dente di cengiaro], then it can quickly throw a thrust or two with advancing steps [accresser di pe'], then deliver a falling strike, ending in that same guard.

24v-d

The Middle Boar's Tusk can do whatever the low one [l'uno tutto] can do. Just as the wild boar strikes diagonally with its tusks, so you strike diagonally with your sword, to displace your opponent's sword. Having uncovered your opponent, from this position you can launch thrusts, or destroy his hands, head or arms.

Forward Guard also called Crown Guard -   fluid
[posta frontale ditta corona -   instable

Middle Boar's Tusk - fixed
[posta di dente zenghiaro mezana - stabile]

* - The text actually reads "pass backwards with the rear foot", which makes no sense. I believe this is a textual error, hence I've translated "indredo" as "front" not "rear".

25r-t

I'm the sword, deadly against all weapons. Neither spear, nor poleaxe, nor dagger can prevail against me. I can strike long or short, or I can be held in the half sword grip to move to the Close Range Game [lo zogho stretto]. I can be used to take away the opponent's sword, or move to grapple. My skill lies in breaking and binding. I'm also skilled in covering and striking, with which I seek always to finish the fight. I'll crush anyone who opposes me. I'm of royal blood. I dispense justice, advance the cause of good and destroy evil. To those who learn my crossings I'll grant great fame and renown in the art of armed fighting.

Long Range Plays [Zogho Largo]

25r-c

Here begin the Long Range plays [zogho largo] of the two handed sword [spada a doy man]. This Master who is crossed at the point of his sword with this player says: "When I'm crossed at the points, I quickly switch my sword to the other side, and strike him from that side with a falling blow to his head or his arms. Alternately, I can place a thrust into his face, as the next picture will show."

25r-d

I've placed a thrust into his face, as the previous Master said. Also, I could've done what he told you, that is, when my sword was crossed on the right I could've quickly switched sides to the left, striking his head or arms with a falling blow."

1st Remedy Master

Student

25v-a

I'm also crossed for the long range game [zogho largo], but this time at the middle of the swords. Immediately after making my cross I let my sword drop down to slide forwards and backwards over his hands. Or, if I choose to pass forward with my right foot and move offline, I can then make a thrust into your chest, as you'll see drawn next.

25v-b

Here you see me completing the play of my teacher. I've made his cover, and then immediately I do what he said to do, that is I strike first to my opponent's arms, and then I continue with a thrust into his chest.

2nd Remedy Master

1st Student

25v-c

My teacher previously instructed me that when I'm crossed at mid-swords with my opponent, I should immediately advance forward and seize his sword as shown, and then strike him with a cut or a thrust. Also I could destroy his leg as you see drawn next, by stomping with my foot against the side of his knee or under the kneecap.

25v-d

As the previous student told you, our teacher taught us this technique. Here I show you how it's done, and as you can see my opponent can do nothing to stop me.

2nd Student

3rd Student

This play is named "The Peasant's Strike" [colpo di villano] and you do it like this: take a narrow stance with your left foot forward, and wait for the peasant to attack first with his sword. When he launches his attack, immediately advance your left foot to your left off the line, and also step sideways to the left with your right foot, receiving his strike in the middle of your sword. Now let his sword slide off yours to the ground, and then quickly counter-attack with a falling strike to his head or arms, or a thrust into his chest as you see drawn in the next picture. This is also a good play if you're fighting sword versus poleaxe, or against a heavy or light staff.

4th Student
The Peasant's Strike [colpo di villano]

In the previous drawing, you saw the Peasant's Strike, in which you saw a thrust well-placed into the attacker's chest. Alternatively, he could have struck a falling blow to the opponent's head or the arms, as I explained p reviously. *Also, if the opponent seeks to counter me by striking back up with a rising blow to my arms from the left, **I quickly advance my left foot and place my sword over his, and from this position he can do nothing to me.

5th Student *Counter, & **Counter-Counter

If your opponent strikes to your leg, withdraw your front foot, or pass backwards and strike downwards to his head, as shown in the drawing. With a two handed sword it's unwise to strike to the knee or below, because it's too dangerous for the one striking. If you attack your opponent's leg, you leave yourself completely uncovered. Now if you've fallen to the ground, then it's all right to strike at your opponent's legs, but otherwise it's not a good idea, as you should generally oppose his sword with your sword.

6th Student

This play, where I strike you with a kick to the groin, is made to hurt you so much that your cover will falter. When you make this play you should do it quickly, to prevent your opponent from being able to counter it. *The counter to this play must be done quickly, and is made by the player grabbing the student's right leg with his left hand, and then throwing him to the ground.

7th Student & *Counter

This play's named "The Exchange of Thrusts" [scambiar de punta], and it's done like this: when your opponent thrusts at you, quickly advance your front foot off the line, and with the other foot step to the side, also moving off the line, crossing his sword with your hands low and your point high into his face, or chest, as you see drawn here.

This play arises from the exchange of thrusts that came before me. If you make the thrust, and your opponent fails to immediately position his point either into your face or into your chest, perhaps because you're in armor, then you should quickly pass forward with your left foot, and seize his sword as shown here. Then strike him hard with your sword, since you have his sword gripped and he cannot escape.

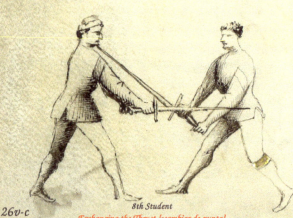

8th Student

Exchanging the Thrust [scambiar de punta]

9th Student

This is another defense you can make against the thrust. When someone thrusts at you as described in the "Exchange of Thrusts", two plays before me [26v-a], then you must advance and step off the line. You should do the same thing in this play, except that in the "Exchange of Thrusts" you thrust back with your hands low and your point high, as I explained earlier. But in this play, which is named "Breaking the Point" [rompere de punta], you proceed with your hands high and as you advance and step off the line you strike downwards, crossing the opponent's thrust at mid-sword, and driving it to the ground. Then you quickly close to grapple.

The student who preceded me beat his opponent's sword to the ground. Now I'm going to complete his play, as follows: after I beat my opponent's sword to the ground I stomp on it with my right foot. This will either break it or prevent him from being able to lift it. But wait— there's more. As soon as I've pinned his sword to the ground with my foot, I strike him with the false edge of my sword under his beard or into his neck. And then immediately I'll return with a falling strike of my sword to his arms or his hands, as you see drawn here.

10th Student

Breaking the Thrust [rompere de punta]

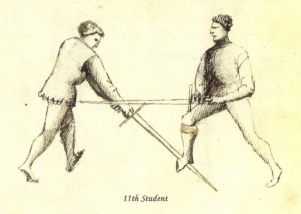

11th Student

Two Handed Sword - Long Range Plays

29

27r-a

Here's another drawing of the "Breaking the Thrust" play, that you saw first two drawings previously [26v-c]. After I've beaten his sword to the ground I quickly pin it to the ground with my right foot, and then strike him in the head, as you see shown here.

27r-b

This is another play that flows from the "Breaking of the Thrust" play. After I've broken his point, if he raises his sword to cover as I strike upwards, I quickly drop the hilt of my sword inside his right arm, near his right hand, then I grab my blade near the point with my left hand, and then strike him in his face. Or alternatively, if I chose, I could drive my sword edge into his neck, slicing him across his throat.

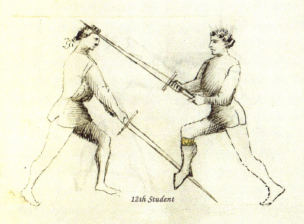

12th Student

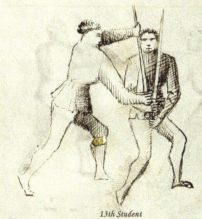

13th Student

27r-c

Also, after I've beaten aside or crossed my opponent's sword, I can press my left hand to his right elbow and push strongly. This will turn him and leave him unprotected, after which I can strike him.

27r-d

The student who preceded me spoke truly when he told you that he could turn the opponent and cut to his head. In addition, before you could turn back to make cover I would give you a major wound in your back with the point of my sword.

14th Student

15th Student

27v-a

This play's named "The False Point" [punta falsa] or "The Short Point" [punta curta], and I'll explain how to do it. I make it look like I'm making a powerful attack against my opponent with a crosswise strike to his head. As he makes cover I strike his sword but only lightly. Then I quickly turn my sword to the other side of his blade, gripping my sword with my left hand at about mid-sword. From there I can quickly make a thrust into his throat or chest. This play however works better in armor than unarmored.

27v-b

This play's the counter to the previous play that was called the "False Point" [punta falsa] or "Short Point" [punta curta], and it's made like this: when the student strikes my sword lightly and then turns his sword around to the other side, I turn my sword around his in exactly the same way, stepping sideways to the left as I do so to gain his unprotected side. From here I can make a thrust into his face. This counter is good both in armor or unarmored.

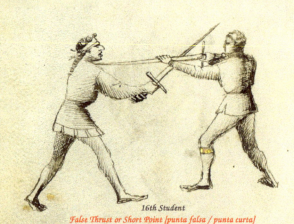

16th Student
False Thrust or Short Point [punta falsa / punta curta]

Counter to 16th Student

Close Range Plays [Zogo Stretto]

27v-c

Here end the Long Range plays [zogho largo] of the two handed sword, made up of plays that are all connected to each other, including remedies and counters from both the right and left sides, and counter-thrusts and counter-cuts to each situation, with breaks, covers, strikes and locks, all of which have been clearly presented.

27v-d

Here we begin the Close Range plays [zogo stretto] of the two handed sword, in which you'll see all manner of covers, strikes, locks, dislocations, sword disarms and throws to the ground. I'll also show the remedies and the counters needed for each situation, whether you're attacking or defending.

30

28r-a

We stand with crossed swords, and from this crossing either one of us can make all of the plays that follow. And as I told you earlier, these plays will follow in sequence.

28r-b

Using the crossing my teacher made with his right foot forward, I now complete the first play as follows: I pass forward with my left foot, and I reach over my right arm with my left hand, seizing his sword-grip in the middle, between his hands. From here I can strike him with either my edge or my point. This grip can be made when fighting with the two-handed sword or the one-handed sword, and I can make this grip by reaching either under or over the crossed swords.

Remedy Master

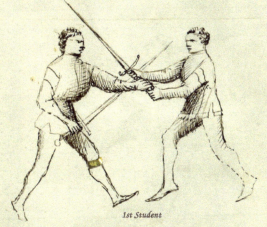

1st Student

28r-c

This is another play that flows from the crossing of my teacher. And from that crossing I can make this play and all of the others that follow. In this play I grip my opponent at the elbow as shown, and then strike him in the face with the pommel of my sword. After that I can also strike him in the head with a falling strike before he has a chance to make cover against me.

28r-d

This is another pommel strike, which is effective against a man in or out of armor. Make this strike quickly if his face is unprotected, and you'll certainly hurt him. I can tell you from experience that with this strike you'll have him spitting out four teeth. From here, if you wish, you can also throw your sword around his neck, as my fellow student will show you next.

2nd Student

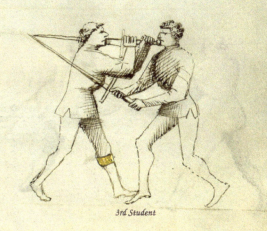

3rd Student

28v-a

As the student who preceded me told you, after doing the previous play I now wrap my sword-edge around your neck. From here, if I discover that you have no neck armor, I'll easily cut your throat.

28v-b

From the crossed swords I pass with cover and bind your arms as shown, then I thrust my sword into your face. Now if I advance the left foot forward, I can bind both your arms. Or, alternately, I can do the play shown next, where I bind your sword by gripping your cross-guard.

4th Student

5th Student

28v-c

Here I'm making the bind that the previous student told you about, and from this position I can strike you with impunity. I have your sword bound by its cross-guard, and from here I can strike you with both cuts and thrusts. In addition, if done quickly this play can defeat all attempts to take my sword, and if it's done quickly enough it will defeat the opponent's close range play.

28v-d

When I'm crossed I move to the Close Range Game [zogho stretto]. I place the hilt of my sword between your two hands, then I push your two hands upwards so that your sword's high. From here I throw my left arm over your arms from the left, binding them with your sword pinned under my left arm. Then I'll strike you multiple times until I'm exhausted. The student who follows me will show you what happens next.

6th Student

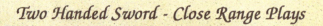

7th Student

31

29r-a

I've now completed the play which I told you about in the previous drawing. Your arms have been bound in a middle bind [ligadura mezana]. Your sword's captured, and can't help you, whereas I can cause you major injury with mine. I can now drive my sword into your neck, quickly moving to the play shown next.

29r-b

This play follows on from the previous one, where the student struck his opponent multiple times while using his left arm to keep the opponent's arms and sword pinned. Now I drive my sword [crossguard] into my opponent's neck as depicted. Then I throw him to the ground to complete the play.

8th Student

9th Student

29r-c

If he covers from his left side, grab his left hand including his pommel with your left hand, and push it upwards and backwards. From there you'll be able to strike him with thrusts and cuts.

29r-d

If he covers from his right side, seize his sword with your left hand as shown and strike him with a thrust or a cut. Then after striking him hard, if you wish, you can drop your own sword and cut his face or neck with his own sword, in the manner shown by the student in the next picture.

10th Student

11th Student

Following on from the play of the student before me, I cut my opponent's face with his own sword, then force him to the ground. Here I'm demonstrating just how effective this art really is.

29v-b

This play's taken from the first play of the First Dagger Remedy Master [10v-a], who places his left hand over the opponent's wrist to take the dagger from his hand. In similar fashion the student here places his left hand over the opponent's right forearm, rotating it outwards to remove the sword from his right hand. Or from here he can transition to a middle bind, as shown in the second play of the above-mentioned First Dagger Remedy Master [10v-c]. That bind also belongs to this student.

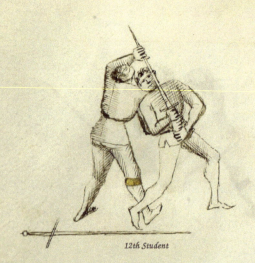

12th Student

13th Student

29v-c

I'm the counter to the student who preceded me, if he tries to use the second play of the First Dagger Remedy Master against me [10v-c] that you heard about previously. This is how I'm done. When I perform this play I doubt you'll be able to keep hold of your sword or remain on your feet.

29v-d

I'm also a counter to the student who tried to use the second play of the First Dagger Remedy Master against me [10v-c]. From the previous picture, if I now start to cut into his throat, he'll stand up a little, and then if I move quickly, I can throw him backwards to the ground.

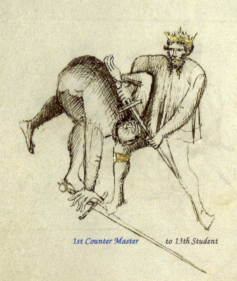

1st Counter Master   to 13th Student

2nd Counter Master to 13th Student

32

30r-a

¶ If I'm crossed at close range [ale strette] with someone, I can quickly make this move to prevent him from attacking me by taking my sword, or applying a lock. I can also strike him with thrusts or cuts without any danger to me.

30r-b

¶ This play's performed as follows: against a crosswise strike from his left, you meet it with a crosswise strike of your own from your left. Then you quickly move to close range under cover, and wrap your sword around your opponent's neck, as you see drawn here. From here you can easily throw him to the ground.

14th Student

15th Student

30r-c

¶ This is the high [sovrano] sword disarm [tor di spada]. With my left hand I pin his hands, while at the same time I press forwards against his blade with the grip of my sword so that he loses his grip on his sword. Then I'll deal him several good strikes. The student who comes after me will show how this play finishes with the opponent's sword lying on the ground.

30r-d

¶ After the disarm performed by the student who came before me, you'll feel your sword fall to the ground. And now there's no question as to whether I can strike you or not.

16th Student

17th Student

30v-a

This is how you do the middle [mezano] sword disarm. The rotation of the opponent's sword is the same as in the first disarm, but the grip on his arm is not the same.

18th Student

30v-b

This is another sword disarm, named the low [sottano] disarm. The low disarm is performed in a similar way to the high disarm, with the same rotation of the opponent's sword, following the same path. With your right hand you press his blade forwards, making his sword handle rotate upwards, and you must keep your left hand on his handle as it turns.

19th Student

30v-c

Here's another way you can take his sword if you're crossed at close range [ale strette]: put your right hand above his and grab his sword at mid-blade keeping it upright, then quickly drop your sword to the ground. Now with your left hand you grab your opponent's sword under the pommel, and turn it to his left. Then your opponent will be forced to immediately release his sword.

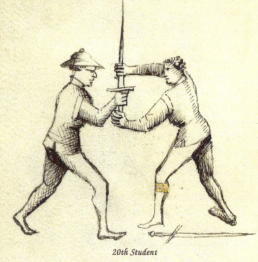

20th Student

Sword vs. Spear

33

31r-a

Here we see three friends who seek to kill this Master, who's waiting for them with his two handed sword. The first intends to throw his sword at the Master like a spear. The second aims to strike him with a cut or a thrust. The third intends to throw two spears he has made ready, as you see drawn here.

31r-b

I wait in this guard—the Boar's Tusk [dente di zenghiaro]—for these three to attack, but I could also wait in other guards, for example, left side Guard of the Lady [posta de donna la senestra] or left side Window Guard [posta di fenestra sinestra], and with any of these I'd be able to defend just as well as I can with the Boar's Tusk. Each of these guards uses the same method of defense. I wait calmly for them to come at me one after the other, and my defense won't fail against cuts, thrusts, nor any handheld weapon they throw at me. I advance my right front foot off the line and with my left I step sideways, beating the incoming weapon aside towards my opponent's left side. And that's how I make my defense: first by making cover and then by quickly counter attacking.

Remedy Master

Staff & Dagger vs. Spear

31r-c

This Master awaits these two men with spears. The Master, who's waiting with a staff and a dagger, sees that the first intends to attack with an overhand strike, while the second intends to strike underhand. In each case, before either opponent attacks with his spear, the Master tilts his staff to the right, like the guard Low Iron Gate [tutta porta di ferro], turning himself without moving his feet or lifting the staff off the ground. And so the Master waits in this guard. As either opponent attacks, the Master pushes the spear aside with his staff to the left, using his dagger too if needed. Following that cover, the Master steps and strikes. Both attackers with their spears will discover that he has a good defense.

31r-d

We were both planning on striking this master, but as you heard we can no longer do that, unless we deceive him [when he blocks our strike] by rotating our spear so that the steel blade is at the rear and then striking him with the spear-butt. Then, if he blocks the butt-strike, we'll rotate our spear again and strike him on his other side with the steel blade. That's how we will counter him..

Remedy Master

Counter to Remedy Master

31v-a

This is the play of the Master who waits for those two men with spears. The Master has a dagger in his right hand, and he holds a staff vertically in front of him in his left hand. He does the play like this - I'll show it for him in his place. *If this player had any skill, he could've avoided the dagger's point. If he'd widened his grip on the spear and had covered by crossing under my dagger with the butt-end of his spear, this would'nt have happened to him. He could've wounded me with his spear if he'd known how to counter me.

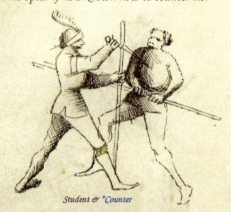

*Student & *Counter*

31v-b

This Master defends with two cudgels against a spear, as follows: when the spear man approaches to attack, the Master throws the cudgel in his right hand at his opponent's head." Then he quickly strikes with the cudgel in his left hand to make cover against the spear, and then he strikes his opponent in the chest with his dagger, as is shown next.

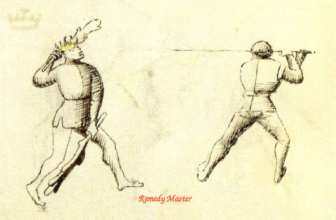

Remedy Master

31v-c

I show the play of the Master before me. *If he'd known the counter, he would've obstructed me as follows: he would've lifted my hands with his spear by rotating it under my dagger, and in that way he would've been able to obstruct me and destroy me. Instead, this is what you get when you know nothing.

*Student & *Counter*

This Master with these swords signifies the seven blows of the sword. And the four animals signify four virtues, namely: prudence [avisamento], speed [presteza], strength [forteza], and boldness [ardimento]. Whoever wants to excel in this art will need to acquire these virtues.

No creature sees better than I the Lynx, and I proceed always with careful calculation.

Prudence   [Avisamento]

I'm the Tiger, and I'm so quick to run and turn, that even the thunderbolt from heaven can't catch me.

No one has a more courageous heart than I, the Lion, for I welcome all to meet me in battle.

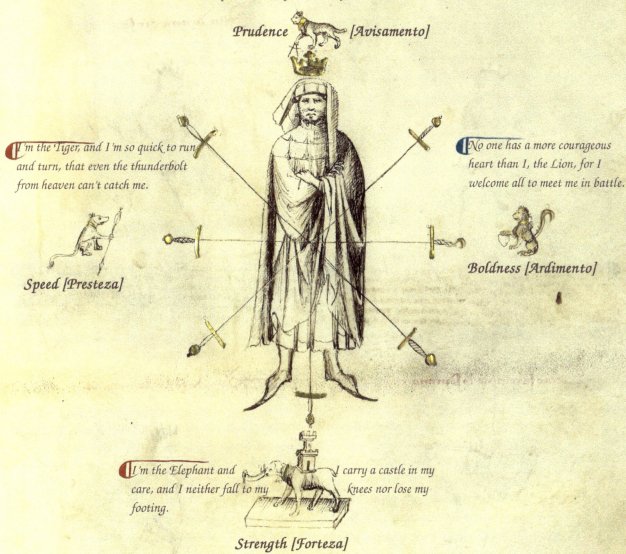

Speed [Presteza]

Boldness [Ardimento]

I'm the Elephant and I carry a castle in my care, and I neither fall to my knees nor lose my footing.

Strength [Forteza]

Chart [Segno]

Armored Sword [Spada en Arme]

32v-a

We're six masters who are very knowledgeable in the art of armed fighting, and each one of us is an expert in this art. Hand-held weapons do not worry us, because we know how to defend against any cuts and thrusts that may come our way. I'm the Short Serpent Guard [posta breve la serpentina], and I consider myself superior to the other guards. When I thrust, those I strike will be well-marked.

Short Serpent Guard
[posta breve la serpentina]

32v-c

I'm the High Serpent Guard [serpentine la soprano] and I'm well positioned to give great underhand thrusts, since I begin high but end low. I'll launch a great thrust into you as I step. That's my skill and I'm good at it. Your cuts don't concern me in the slightest, because when it's time to hand out great thrusts, you'll get more than your fair share from me.

High Serpent Guard
[serpentine la soprano]

32v-b

I choose to use the Guard of the True Cross [posta di vera crose] against you. And your thrust will fail to strike me. I'll make cover to your attack as I make my step, and my thrust will never fail to strike you. Neither you nor the other guards concern me, because I'm so well versed in the art of armed fighting that my crossing will never fail me. Step, cross swords, then strike, and this art will never fail you.

Guard of the True Cross
[posta de vera crose]

32v-d

I'm named Middle Iron Gate [porto di ferro la mezana], and whether you're armored or unarmored I make strong thrusts. I step offline with my left foot and I put a thrust into your face. I can also place my point and blade between your arms in such a way that I'll put you into the middle bind [10v-c], as shown and discussed earlier.

Middle Iron Gate
[porto di ferro la mezana]

33r-a

I'm known as the Archer's Guard [posta sagittaria], and I throw great thrusts as I step offline. If strikes or thrusts come against me, I make a strong cover, then immediately strike with my counter. This is my skill, and I never vary from it.

The Archer's Guard [posta sagittaria]

33r-b

I'm the Mixed Guard of the Cross [posta di crose bastarda], and I'm related to the Guard of the True Cross, in that anything it can do, I can do also. I make strong covers, thrusts or cuts, usually avoiding your strike by stepping offline, and my strikes are my greatest asset.

Mixed Guard of the Cross [posta de crose bastarda]

33r-c

This cover is made from the Guard of the True Cross [posta di vera crose], when I step diagonally offline. And so you can see what can be done from this cover, my students, who are experienced in mortal combat, will demonstrate their skills and show the plays that immediately follow it.

Remedy Master

33r-d

I'm the first student of the Master who came before me, and I make this thrust from his cover. You should also know that you can make this thrust from both the Guard of the True Cross and the Mixed Guard of the Cross. As the opponent makes his thrust, the Master, or his student who's waiting in either of these guards (or positions), keeps his body low and steps offline, crossing the opponent's sword with his point high into the opponent's face or chest and the hilt of his sword kept low, as shown here.

1st Student

33v-a

If I see my thrust can't penetrate his chest or his face due to his visor, I can lift his visor to thrust into his face. And if this doesn't satisfy me, I can apply other stronger plays.

33v-b

When I closed with this opponent, his armor prevented me from striking him as shown in the previous play. So instead I push strongly against his elbow and make him turn away. Let's see now if his armor is strong enough when he's attacked from behind.

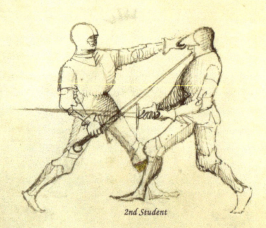

2nd Student

3rd Student

33v-c

When I saw my sword was ineffective against you, I quickly applied this grappling technique. I believe your armor will be useless to you when I put you in this strong lower bind [ligadura de sotto], which is shown further in the next picture.

33v-d

I have you locked in the lower bind [ligadura de sotto] or "strong key" [chiave forte], and from this position you can't escape regardless of how strong you are. I could hurt you or even kill you. I could stop to write a letter and you wouldn't even be able to see what I was doing. You've lost your sword and your helmet, you've been humiliated, and you'll soon be hurting.

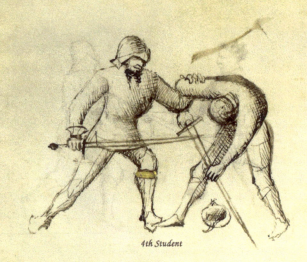

4th Student

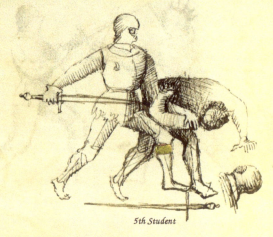

5th Student

34r-a

This play flows from the first Master who showed the Guard of the True Cross [posta di vera crose] or the Mixed Guard of the Cross [bastarda], as follows: when the opponent makes a thrust at the student who is waiting in guard, the student quickly steps off line to make cover, and counters with a thrust to the opponent's face. Then the student advances his left foot behind his opponent's lead foot as shown, in order to throw him to the ground, using the point of his sword to hook around his opponent's neck.

34r-b

When I move from my guard to a close range cover [la covert stretta], and I'm unable to strike you with a cut, I'll strike you with a thrust. If I cannot strike you with either, I'll strike you with the cross guard or with the pommel, depending on my preference. Also, if I choose to play at close range [ale strette], and my opponent believes I intend to use my sword, I'll switch to grappling if this gives me an advantage, or, if not, I can strike him in the face with my cross guard as I told you before, whichever I like.

6th Student

7th Student

34r-c

As you saw, the student who preceded me struck his opponent in the face with the crossguard of his sword. After that he can quickly strike him in the face with his pommel, as you see depicted below.

34r-d

Let me also tell you that the student immediately before me who struck his opponent in the face with the pommel of his sword could also have done what I do, that is, step with his right foot behind his opponent's left leg, and then hook his opponent's neck with his sword handle, to throw him to the ground as I do here.

8th Student

9th Student

34v-a

This play also flows from the Guard of the True Cross, like this: when a student is in that guard, and an opponent comes against him and suddenly attacks him, then the student should step off the line [for a de strada] and thrust his sword point into his face as you see me do here.

34v-b

Let me also point out that if the Student has moved to close range [ale stretta], and finds himself unable to destroy his opponent with his sword, then he should use his sword to grapple as shown, that is, he should wrap his sword around his opponent's neck, then step with his right foot behind the opponent's left foot, and throw him to the ground to the right.

10th Student

11th Student

34v-c

This student's unable to strike his opponent effectively, so he transitions to grappling as follows: he places his sword point to the inside of his opponent's right arm. Then the student slides his sword and his left arm under the opponent's right arm, to throw him to the ground, or lock him in the lower bind [ligadura de sotto], also known as the "strong key" [chiave forte].

34v-d

This is a good strong grappling move. As he makes his grip on the opponent's right arm, the student steps with his left foot behind his opponent's left foot, and thrusts the point of his sword into his face. He can also throw his opponent to the ground to the student's right.

12th Student

13th Student

35r-a

This is the counter to the Remedy Master and all his students. It's generally true that every counter you use against a Remedy Master will also break the plays of all that Remedy Master's students. And this is true for the spear, poleaxe, sword, dagger, and grappling, that is, for the entire art. Let me return to address the Remedy Master: when he's making his cover, the Counter-Remedy Master places his left hand behind his opponent's right elbow and gives it a powerful push, turning him in order to strike him from behind, as you see drawn next.

35r-b

I'm the student of the Counter-Remedy Master who came before me, and I complete his play as follows: when I've turned my opponent, I immediately strike him from behind, either under his right arm, under his coif into the back of his head, into his buttocks (excuse my language), or into the back of his knee, or into any other target where he's unprotected.

Counter Master to Remedy Master

Student of the Counter Master

35r-c

This sword can be used as a sword or a poleaxe, and should not be sharpened from the guard down to one hand's-width from the point. The point should be sharp and the sharp edge should be about a hand's-width in length. The roundel below the hilt should be able to slide down the blade to a hand's-width from the point and no further. The hilt needs to be strongly made with a heavy pommel with well-tempered spikes. The spikes should be well-tempered and sharp. The front of the sword should be as heavy as the back, and the weight should be from three and a half to five and a half pounds, depending on how big and strong the man is and how he chooses to arm himself.

35r-d

This other sword is fully sharpened from the hilt all the way to the point, except there is an unsharpened section in the middle about a hand's width, big enough for a gloved hand to be able to hold it there. Just like the previous sword, this sword should be sharp with a fine point, and the hilt should be strong with a heavy pommel and a sharp well-tempered spike.

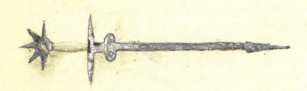

Armored Poleaxe[Azza]

35v-a

I'm the Short Serpent Guard [posta breve la Serpentina] and I consider myself superior to the other guards. Whoever receives one of my thrusts will be scarred for life. This guard delivers a powerful thrust that can penetrate cuirasses and breastplates. Fight with me if you want me to prove it.

Short Serpent Guard [poste breve la serpentina]

35v-b

I'm named the Guard of the True Cross [posta di vera crose], because I defend myself by crossing weapons, and the entire art of fencing and armed combat is based on defending yourself by covering with crossed weapons. Strike as you wish, I'll be waiting for you, and with a step and a thrust of my pole-axe, I can do just as the student of the First Remedy Master of the sword in armor does [33r-d].

Guard of the True Cross [posta de vera crose]

35v-c

I'm the Guard of the Lady [posta de donna], and I go against the Boar's Tusk guard [dente zenghiaro]. If I see him waiting for me, I'll make a powerful strike at him, in which I move my left foot off the line, and pass forwards, striking downwards at his head. If he blocks strongly under my poleaxe with his, then even if I can't strike him in his head I'll not fail to strike his arms or hands.

Guard of the Lady [posta de donna]

35v-d

If my Middle Iron Gate [porta di ferro mezana] guard is opposed by the Guard of the Lady [posta di donna], we both know each other's game, for we've faced each other many, many times in battle with swords and with poleaxes. And let me tell you, what she claims she can do to me, I can do better against her. Also let me tell you that if I had a sword instead of a poleaxe, then I'd thrust it into my opponent's face as follows: when I'm waiting in the Middle Iron Gate with my two-handed sword, if he attacks me with his poleaxe with a powerful falling strike from the Guard of the Lady, then I quickly advance forward striking him strongly under his poleaxe as I step off the line, and then I quickly grasp my sword in the middle with my left hand and make the thrust into his face. While there is little difference between we two guards, I'm the more deceptive of the two.

Middle Iron Gate [porta di ferro mezana]

36r-a

I'm the Long Tail Guard [coda longa], used against the Window Guard [posta de fenestra], and I can strike at any time. With my falling strikes I can beat every poleaxe or sword to the ground, setting me up nicely for close play [zogo stretto]. As you observe the plays that follow, please consider each one in sequence.

36r-b

I'm named Window Guard [posta de fenestra] on the left, and I'm made with the right arm pulled back. This is not a good guard to wait in. Everything I do is deceptive. You think that I'm going to launch a falling strike, but I pass backwards and switch guards. So while I began on the left, I actually enter on the right. I can also quickly transition to the plays that follow.

Long Tail Guard [coda longa]

Window Guard on the left [posta de fenestra sinestra]

36v-a

These are the put the above guards to the test. Each guard can do them, and each guard believes it will prevail. As is drawn here, whoever beats his opponent's poleaxe to the ground can do these plays, and will succeed if his opponent fails to counter him.

36v-b

This student puts his axe between his opponent's legs, and covers his eyes with his left hand. When the opponent, who cannot see, tries to turn, he'll surely fall to the ground.

1st Student

2nd Student

36v-c

The previous student can also do this play when he's at close range, as you can see here. He steps with his left foot on top of his opponent's poleaxe head, and draws back his own poleaxe, then thrusts it into his opponent's face.

36v-d

The previous student sees that it isn't possible to strike his opponent in the face with his poleaxe, because his opponent's visor is too strong. So he advances his left foot forward, lifts the opponent's visor, and drives his point into his face with as much force as he can give to his poleaxe. You can add on this play to any of the previous plays, as well as to any of the plays which follow.

3rd Student

4th Student

37r-a

With this hold I can strike you in the head with my poleaxe, and with my left arm I'll put you in the strong lower bind [ligadura de sotto], which is more deadly than any other lock.

37r-b

With a half-turn of this poleaxe I'll take it from your hands. Once I've taken it from you with this turn, I'll strike you in the head with it, as the next student shows. I don't believe you will survive this.

5th Student

6th Student

37r-c

This play follows on from the student before me. As he clearly told you, you'll likely drop dead to the ground after being struck in the head like this. If this blow is not enough then I can give you another, and, if I choose, I can also drag you to the ground by your visor, which is drawn next.

37r-d

I'm demonstrating what the student before me said he would do to you, that is, dragging you to the ground by your visor. This is one of the better grappling techniques you can do.

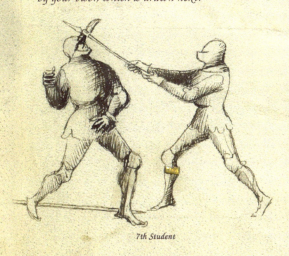

7th Student

8th Student

37v-a

This play is easy to understand, and you can clearly see how I can drag him to the ground. When I have him on the ground, I can drag him behind me. And when the long tail of my poleaxe can no longer hold him, then he'll feel my strikes.

37v-b

This poleaxe of mine is filled with a powder and is hollow and perforated. This powder is so strongly corrosive that the moment it touches your eye, you'll no longer be able to open it, and you may be permanently blinded.

I'm the poleaxe, heavy, vicious, and deadly. I deliver blows more powerful than any other hand-held weapon. If my first strike misses, then my poleaxe becomes risky to hold on to and is of no more use to me. But if my first blow is powerfully made on target, then I can stop any other hand-held weapon. If I 'm accompanied with good protective armor, then I can defend myself with any of the powerful striking guards of the sword. My most noble lord, my Marquis, there are some vicious things shown in this book that I know you would never do. I show you them purely to aid your knowledge.

Remedy Master

Remedy Master

37v-d

This is the powder that you use in the poleaxe drawn above. Take the sap of the spurge, and dry it in a warm oven to make a powder. Now take two ounces of this powder and one ounce of powder of victim flower, and mix them together. Now load this powder into the poleaxe shown above. You can do this with any good caustic powder, but you won't find a better recipe than the one in this book.

Armored Spear [Lanza]

39r-a

[We're three masters using spear guards that are closely related to the sword guards. I'm the first, which is the *Low Iron Gate [tutta porta di ferro]*. I'm positioned to quickly beat aside my opponent's spear, and to do that I step sideways off the line with my right foot, crossing his spear and beating it to the left. When you step and beat aside together, that combination is hard to beat.

Low Iron Gate [tutta porta di ferro]

39r-c

[I'm positioned in the *Middle Iron Gate [mezza porta di ferro]*. My method is to beat aside, then counter-strike. Come against me as you like with short spear or staff, but when I beat your weapon aside as I step I'll never fail to strike you. When you're using a short spear or sword, all guards that are made with the point offline are sufficient for you to wait in when facing any long hand-held weapon. Guards that cover from the right are followed with a step and a thrust. Guards from the left side can also cover and beat aside, but these will wound with a strike, because they can't effectively place a thrust.

Middle Iron Gate [meza porta di ferro]

39v-a

I'm the noble right side Window Guard [posta di finestra destra], always ready to beat aside and counter-strike, and a long spear hardly bothers me. Also, if I was using a sword I'd wait for the long spear in this same guard that can beat aside and obstruct all thrusts. I can also exchange thrusts, or beat them to the ground without difficulty. I'd finish this play with the play shown next.

Right side Window Guard [posta di finestra destra]

Student

39v-c

The three guards shown above - Low Iron Gate, Middle Iron Gate and the high right side Window Guard - should all finish with this strike, which is used to end the play and demonstrates their skill. Here I show the finishing strike for each of them.

39v-d

This is the counter to the three spear masters shown above, who all finish their play with the strike shown above. Let me explain how to do it: When the Master believes he has driven my spear off-line, I rotate my spear and I'll strike him with the butt end, which is steel-capped, like the point. Thus, the plays of these Masters pose little threat to me.

Counter to Right Spear Masters

40r-a

We're three left side guards, and I'm the first, which is the Boar's Tusk. The left side guards work the same as the right side guards. We step offline advancing our lead foot, and then we strike with our thrusts on the left side. Both right side and left side guards first beat aside, and then thrust, because other attacks with the spear are not as effective.

40r-b

I'm waiting for you in the Guard of the True Cross [posta di vera crose]. You've clearly approached too close to me. I'll pass backwards with my leading right foot, beating your spear offline to my right. My thrust won't fail me. Yours on the other hand will fail you.

Boar's Tusk [dente di zenghiaro]

Guard of the True Cross [posta di vera crose]

40r-c

I'm positioned in the left side Window Guard [fenestra sinistra]. If I don't strike you with a thrust you can count yourself lucky. I'll step offline to the left with my left foot, with my point held high and my arms low. Then I'll thrust into your face and you'll have no defense. The play that follows is the finish used by all three Masters. If you try it once, you won't need to try it again.

40r-d

Here we end the plays of the spear that are made from the left side against threats and attacks. These three guards shown above are carefully chosen to easily defeat the long or the short spear, since they're effective in offense or defense. *The counter to this thrust is easily done: when your thrust is beaten offline, you turn the butt of your spear and strike with that. And with that I've now shown you enough of the plays of the spear.

left side Window Guard [posta de fenestra sinistra]

Student & *Counter

Blank

Fighting On Horseback

41r-a

I carry my lance in the Boar's Tusk guard [dente di cenghiaro], because I'm well-armored and have a shorter lance than my opponent. My intention is to beat his lance offline as I raise mine diagonally, and this will result in our lances crossing each other at about an arm's length from the point. My lance however will then run into his body, while his will pass offline and miss me. And that's how this one is done. This text applies to the drawing on the right.

Boar's Tusk guard [dente di cenghiaro]

41r-c

This is the counter to the previous play when one person rides against another with sharp steel, and where one has a shorter lance than the other. When he who has the shorter lance carries it low in the Boar's Tusk, then he with the longer lance should similarly carry his lance low, as drawn here, so that the short lance can't beat aside the long lance.

Counter Master to Boar's Tusk

41v-b

This is another way to carry your lance when fighting another lance. This Master has a short lance, so he carries it in left side Guard of the Lady [poste de donna la sinistra] as you can see, so he can beat aside his opponent's weapon and strike him.

Left side Guard of the Lady [poste de donna la sinistra]

41v-d

This Master also carries his lance in Guard of the Lady on the left, to knock aside the spear his opponent is about to throw at him. Just as he can beat it aside using his lance, so too he could beat it aside using a staff or a short sword.

Left side Guard of the Lady [poste de donna la sinistra]

42r-b

This master who's fleeing isn't wearing armor and rides a horse built for speed, and as he flees he constantly thrusts his lance point behind him to strike at his opponent. If he were to turn his horse to the right, he could quickly enter into the Boar's Tusk [dente di zenghiaro] guard with his lance, or he could take the left side Guard of the Lady [posta di donna la sinistra], to beat aside his opponent's weapon and finish him in similar fashion to the first [41r-a] and the third [41v-b] plays of the lance.

Remedy Master

42r-d

This method of carrying the sword against the lance is well suited for beating aside your opponent's lance when you're passing him on his right side. This guard is effective against all hand-held weapons, including pole axe, staff, sword etc.

Sword vs. Lance Remedy Master

Fighting On Horseback - Lance / Sword vs. Lance 42r

44

42v-a

This is the counter to the previous play. This Master attacks with his lance held low in order to strike his opponent's horse either in the head or the chest, and the opponent will be unable to beat aside such a low attack with his sword.

Counter Master to Sword vs. Lance Remedy Master

42v-d

This is another counter of lance versus sword. In this one, the man with the lance couches his lance under his left arm, so that his lance can't be beaten aside. And in this way he'll be able to strike the man with the sword with his lance.

Counter Master to Sword vs. Lance Remedy Master

Here the man with the sword is waiting for the man with the lance, and he's waiting in the Boar's Tusk [dente di cenghiaro] guard. As the man with the lance approaches him, the Master with the sword beats aside the lance to the right side, covering and striking with one turn of the sword.

Boar's Tusk [dente di cenghiaro]

43r-c

This is the counter to the preceding play of lance versus sword. Here the man with the lance strikes his opponent's (the man with the sword) horse in the head, and the man with the sword is holding his sword too low to beat aside the lance.

Counter Master to Boar's Tusk

This way of carrying the sword is named The Long Tail Guard [posta de coda longa]. When you're riding to your opponent's right side, this is a very good guard to use against the lance and all other hand held weapons. Keep firmly in your mind that thrusts and strikes from the left side should be beaten aside to your outside line, beating them diagonally upwards, not vertically. And the falling strikes should similarly be beaten aside to the outside, lifting your opponent's sword va little as you do so. You make these plays the way these drawings show you.

Long Tail Guard [posta de coda longa]

This version of the Long Tail Guard [guardia de choda longa] is a good guard when your opponent attacks you from his sword on his left shoulder, as this opponent is shown doing here. Be advised that this guard will work against all attacks from both the right and the left sides, and against right handers or left handers alike. Here follow the plays from the Long Tail, and they always begin with beating aside the opponent's weapon, as you saw drawn in the first guard of the Long Tail [43v-b].

Long Tail Guard [posta de coda longa]

46

44r-a

This is the first play that comes from the Long Tail Guard [guardia de coda longa] shown above. Here the Master beats aside his opponent's sword, and then places a thrust into his chest or his face, as you see drawn here.

44r-b

This is the second play that you can do after beating aside your opponent's weapon. Here, seeing his head is unarmored, I strike this man in the head.

1st Student

2nd Student

44r-c

This is another play, the third, where, after beating aside your opponent's sword, you grab it with your left hand and strike him in the head. You could also strike him with a thrust.

44r-d

This is the fourth play, in which the student strikes his opponent in the head and then takes his sword, in the manner shown here.

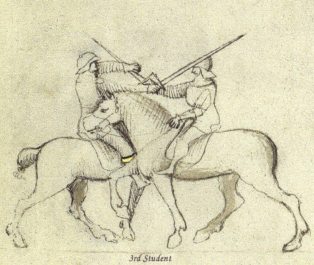

3rd Student

4th Student

44v-a

This is the fifth play that flows from the cover where you beat aside his sword. Here I throw my arm around his neck and turn quickly, and with the base of my sword I drive him to the ground. *My counter's the second play that follows me [44v-c], but this counter won't work if your opponent is armored.

44v-b

This is the sixth play, where you take away your opponent's sword. You use the hilt of your sword to lift his hilt upwards, which will make his sword fall from his hands.

*5th Student & *Counter*

6th Student

44v-c

This is the seventh play, which is the counter to the fifth play above. It uses a strike to your opponent's leg. But if your opponent is armored, you can't trust this counter to work.

44v-d

This is the eighth play, which is the counter to all the preceding plays, but especially the plays of the mounted sword when the Masters are using the Long Tail guard. When the Masters or their students are in this guard, then when I strike or thrust at them, and when they quickly beat my attack aside, then I quickly turn my sword and strike them in the face with my pommel. Then I move quickly from my position, and strike them in the back of the head with a horizontal backhand strike.

Counter Master to 5th Student

Counter Master to all preceding plays

47

45r-a

I'm the ninth play, which is the counter to the counter that preceded me. When he turns his sword, I quickly place my hilt as you see drawn here, so that he can't strike me in the face with his pommel. If I raise my sword up, and turn it to the left, you could well have your sword taken away. But if I'm unable to do that, I could instead strike you with a backhand strike to the face, or with a quick turn of my sword I could strike you in the head with my pommel. Here end the plays of sword against sword on horseback. If you know more about this subject, feel free to share it.

Counter-Counter to Counter of all preceding plays

45r-b

This is a grappling play, that is, a play using your arms, and this is how you do it: if your opponent is fleeing from you, you come up behind him to his left side. Now with your right hand you grab the visor of his bascinet, or if he's unarmored, you grab him by the hair or by the right arm from behind his shoulder. In this way, you'll make him fall backwards to the ground.

1st Student of Grappling

45r-c

This is the counter to the previous play, and that play won't work when this counter is quickly applied, as follows: when he grabs you from behind, you quickly switch hands on the reins, and with your left hand you lock him up, as shown here.

Counter Master to 1st Student of Grappling

45r-d

This student is about to throw his opponent off his horse, by grabbing the stirrup and pulling it upwards. If the opponent doesn't fall to the ground, he'll be helpless in the air, and unless the opponent is tied to his horse, this play won't fail the student. If he doesn't have his foot in the stirrup, the student can grab him by the ankle and lift him up into the air in the same way, as I described above.

2nd Student of Grappling

45v-a

Here's the counter to the previous play: when your opponent grabs your stirrup or your foot, throw your arm quickly around his neck, and in this way, you'll be able to unhorse him. Follow this advice and he'll end up on the ground for sure.

Counter Master to 2nd Student of Grappling

45v-b

This is a method of throwing your opponent to the ground by throwing his horse. It's done like this: when you and your mounted opponent close, ride to his right side. Then throw your right arm over the neck of his horse, and grab the bridle close to where the bit enters its mouth, and f orcefully wrench it upwards and over. At the same time make sure your horse's shoulders drive into his horse's haunches. In this way, you'll bring down both him and his horse at the same time.

3rd Student of Grappling

45v-c

This is the counter to the play before, where you throw both your opponent and his horse to the ground. This is an easy counter: when the student throws his arm over the neck of your horse to grab the bridle, you should quickly throw your arm around the student's neck, and you'll effectively make him let go. Just do as the drawing shows.

Counter Master to 3rd Student of Grappling

45v-d

In this play you take the reins of your opponent's horse out of his hands, as you see drawn here. When you and your mounted opponent close, ride to his right side, and throw your right arm over his horse's neck and grab the reins near his left hand with your right hand turned down. Now pull the reins over his horse's head. This play is safer to do in armor than unarmored.

4th Student of Grappling

46r-a

Here are three opponents who wish to kill this Master. The first intends to strike underhand, and he holds his spear at the mid-point. The second carries his lance couched and fully extended. The third intends to throw his spear. They've agreed that no one will make more than one strike each. They've also agreed to take turns.

46r-b

48

Attack me one after another if you choose, because I'm not going anywhere. I'm ready and waiting for you in the Boar's Tusk guard [dente di cenghiaro]. When the spear is launched against me, whether held tightly or thrown from the hand, I quickly advance my right foot off the line and step crosswise with my left foot, and beat aside the spear that comes to strike me. Even if I were attacked a thousand times, my defense would never once fail me. What I can do with my winged spear [ghiavarina], I could also do with a staff or a sword. Likewise I could also use the defense I make against the spear, against a sword or a staff. My plays are shown next.

Boar's Tusk guard [dente di cenghiaro]

46r-c

This is the play of the Master who waits with his winged spear [ghiavarina] in the Boar's Tusk [dente di cenghiaro] guard, for an attack from the three on horseback. To do this play he steps off line and beats aside his opponent's spear. And even if my opponent may know this play, I'll show him my spear is so fast, that I can strike my opponent with either thrusts or cuts against his head.

46r-d

This is another play made by the Master above, who waits in the Boar's Tusk guard [posta de dente de zenghiaro]. In his place I'll show this play instead of the previous: if he beats aside my spear with his spear, I rotate my spear and strike him with the butt, which is capped with well-tempered steel.

1st Student

2nd Student

46v-a

This Master has bound one end of a strong rope to his horse's saddle, and the other end to the butt of his lance. First he strikes his opponent, then he'll throw the lance to the left side of his opponent, over his opponent's left shoulder, and in this way he can drag his opponent from his horse.

Remedy Master

46v-c

This scoundrel was fleeing from me towards a castle. I rode so hard and fast at full rein that I caught up with him near his castle. Then I struck him with my sword in his armpit, which is a difficult area to protect with armor. Now I'll withdraw, to avoid retaliation from his friends.

46v-d

Here ends this book written by Fiore the student, who has published here everything he knows about this art, by which I mean everything he knows about armed fighting is contained within this book. This same Fiore has named his book "The Flower of the Battle". Let he for whom this book was made be forever praised, for his nobility and virtue have no equal. Fiore the Friulian, a simple elderly man, now entrusts this book to you.

49

Blank

CPSIA information can be obtained
at www.ICGtesting.com
Printed in the USA
BVHW052220310122
627628BV00002B/48